CHILD SOLDIERS

CHILD SOLDIERS

The Role of Children in Armed Conflict

ilene cohn
&
guy s. goodwin-gill

A Study for the Henry Dunant Institute
Geneva

CLARENDON PRESS · OXFORD
1994

Oxford University Press, Walton Street, Oxford OX2 6DP

Oxford New York

Athens Auckland Bangkok Bombay
Calcutta Cape Town Dar es Salaam Delhi
Florence Hong Kong Istanbul Karachi
Kuala Lumpur Madras Madrid Melbourne
Mexico City Nairobi Paris Singapore
Taipei Tokyo Toronto
and associated companies in
Berlin Ibadan

Oxford is a trade mark of Oxford University Press 1994

Published in the United States
by Oxford University Press Inc., New York

British Library Cataloguing in Publication Data
Data available

Library of Congress Cataloging in Publication Data
Data available
ISBN 0–19–825935–2
ISBN 0–19–825932–8 (Pbk.)

1 3 5 7 9 10 8 6 4 2

Printed and bound in Great Britain
on acid-free paper by
Biddles Ltd, Guildford and King's Lynn

Preface & Acknowledgements

THERE IS NO DOUBT IN OUR MINDS that this Study truly springs from the initiative and unfailing support of two people in particular, Kristina Hedlund Thulin, Head of the International Department, Swedish Red Cross, and Jakobina Thordardottir, Head of the International Department, Icelandic Red Cross. How this work began is described more fully in Chapter 1, but the successful completion of this project owes much to their drive and encouragement.

We are also particularly grateful for the considerable financial support provided by both the Swedish and Icelandic Red Cross Societies, without which much of the field work and research could not have been accomplished. Other important contributions for which we are especially appreciative came from the Canadian, Colombian, Danish, Finnish, Japanese and Norwegian Red Cross Societies, the International Committee of the Red Cross and the Oak Foundation.

The fact that a child today should decide or be compelled to take up arms, to kill or be killed, is shocking enough, but less surprising is the fact that such a large number of dedicated people are presently involved in trying to bring the practice to end, or to cope with the after-effects. It has been our good fortune to be able to work or have contact with many of those most actively engaged. Dorothea Woods, of the Quaker United Nations Office, Geneva, contributed to early work on the study. María Teresa Dutli, Legal Officer in the International Committee of the Red Cross, was a constant source of help and encouragement throughout, and also participated in our reference group. The International Committee of the Red Cross (ICRC), with so many humanitarian responsibilities in this age of conflict, was likewise generous in its support. ICRC Legal Advisers, Desk Officers and Delegation staff helped arrange field missions to Liberia, Sri Lanka and Israel and the occupied territories. Despite the pressure on their time, ICRC delegations readily provided much helpful information in their replies to our questionnaires, with important contributions also from the International Federation of Red Cross and Red Crescent Societies and many individual National Red Cross and Red Crescent Societies.

About half way through our efforts, drafts were put before an informal 'reference group' which met in Geneva in January 1993. Their views and practical experience, together with two days of lively discussion, greatly assisted us in organizing and presenting the material. Very special thanks are due to Vesna Bosnjak, of UNICEF, Margaret McCallin, of the International Catholic Child

Bureau, Joanne Tortorici, psychologist, Nicaragua, and Philip Veerman, Co-ordinator of Defence for Children International—Israel, all of whom travelled many miles to be with us. Also present on this occasion, and ever ready and willing to provide help and advice, were Marco Sassoli, Legal Advisor; Denis Noel, Legal Advisor for Africa, and Aldo Benini, Desk Officer for Liberia, all of the International Committee of the Red Cross. Courtney M. O'Connor, Legal Officer, United Nations High Commissioner for Refugees, read the drafts, and we are grateful to all for their constructive comments.

The Annex on treaty ratifications, voting, military age and conscription owes much to the energy and dedication of four students from Canada, Nicola Angelini, Daphné Cousineau, Valérie Héroux, and Jean-François Savoie. Their success in the 1992 Jean Pictet prize brought them to Geneva for a period of intensive work, together with their supervisor, Lise S. Boudreault, for which we are most grateful. Additional information was provided by students at Columbia University Law School, New York; thanks to Renee Harrison, Mike Fried and Enock Chikweche. For help with photo research, thanks to Kieran Eustacz at Associated Press, Priscilla P. Stadler at Impact Visuals, Carrie Chalmers at Magnum Photos, Cathy Cesario Tardosky at Sygma Photo News, Devon Taylor at UNICEF, all in New York; to Champong Lo, ICRC, and Anneliese Hollman, UNHCR, Geneva; and Ian Trevethick, of Redruth, Cornwall.

John Whelan at Oxford University Press brought the study rapidly and enthusiastically to publication, while Larry Breker of LB Publishing, Toronto, performed a masterly job with layout and design, uncomplainingly keeping up with and sometimes ahead of changes and additions.

Finally, we owe much to the friendly and supportive atmosphere of the Henry Dunant Institute in Geneva. Special thanks to Chantal Levet, Nancy Dupont, Daniela Egger, Graziano Baratti and Linnie Kessely for helping to lighten the task of researching and writing an otherwise harrowing topic. A very special measure of gratitude, however, is due to Dr. Jirí Toman, Acting Director of the Institute. This project has been close to his heart throughout our work, and his regular advice, steadfast support and effectiveness in overcoming funding and administrative obstacles helped us considerably in bringing the Study to a successful conclusion. Notwithstanding the broad range of individual and institutional assistance provided to us, this work and the conclusions we draw, like any errors of omission or commission, remain very much our own. We have tried to describe a representative sample of situations of conflict in different regions where child soldiers are involved, and we hope that the information and suggestions will be of interest and assistance to those working at both practical and policy levels. The views expressed are our own, however, and are not necessarily shared by any of the organizations, institutions or individuals with whom we have worked or been in contact.

Guy S. Goodwin-Gill   Ilene Cohn
Geneva, December 1993

Contents

Selected Abbreviations

AFL	Armed Forces of Liberia
API	1977 Additional Protocol I to the 1949 Geneva Conventions
APII	1977 Additional Protocol II to the 1949 Geneva Conventions
CERJ	(Guatemala) Council of Ethnic Communities
CRC	1989 United Nations Convention on the Rights of the Child
CUC	(Guatemala) Peasant Unity Committee
ECOSOC	United Nations Economic and Social Council
EPLF	Eritrean Peoples Liberation Front
ERP	(El Salvador) People's Revolutionary Army (one of five FMLN factions)
FAM	Armed Forces of Mozambique
FMLN	(El Salvador) Farabundo Marti National Liberation Front
GC1	First Geneva Convention of 12 August 1949
GC2	Second Geneva Convention of 12 August 1949
GC3	Third Geneva Convention of 12 August 1949
GC4	Fourth Geneva Convention of 12 August 1949
ICRC	International Committee of the Red Cross

INPFL	Independent National Patriotic Front of Liberia (splinter group of NPFL under Prince Johnson)
IRA	(Ireland) Irish Republican Army
JVP	(Sri Lanka) Janatha Vimukthe Peramuna (Movement)
LOIC	Liberian Opportunities Industrialization Center
LTTE	(Sri Lanka) Liberation Tiger of Tamil Eelam
NGE	Non-government entity
NGO	Non-government organization
NPA	(Philippines) New People's Army
NPFL	National Patriotic Front of Liberia (Charles Taylor)
NRA	(Uganda) National Resistance Army
NRC	(Liberia) National Reconciliation Commission
ONUSAL	United Nations Observer Mission for El Salvador
PAC	(Guatemala) Civilian Defence Patrols
PLO	Palestine Liberation Organization
POW	Prisoner of War
RENAMO	Mozambican Resistance Organization
SPLA	Sudan Peoples Liberation Army
UN	United Nations
UNHCR	United Nations High Commissioner for Refugees
UNICEF	United Nations Children's Fund
UNLA	Uganda National Liberation Army

Yann Gamblin – UNICEF
Uganda, 1986. 12-year old NRA soldier rests between marches.

Steve McCurry – MAGNUM
Afghanistan, 1986.

Robles – AP Photo
Torola River, El Salvador, 1984. 13-year old on guard.

M. Boisard – ICRC
Yemen, 1964.

Patrick Robert – SYGMA
Monrovia, Liberia. October 1990. Prince Johnson's escort.

Patrick Robert – SYGMA
Congotown near Monrovia, Liberia. 9 August 1990. Young
member of Charles Taylor's NPFL.

Donna DeCesare – IMPACT VISUALS
El Salvador, February 1991. Young government soldier.

Jeff Perkell – IMPACT VISUALS
Nicaragua, October 1989. Young government soldier on patrol.

Dexter Cruez – AP Photo
Batticaloa, Sri Lanka, 1990. Tiger Cubs in the bush.

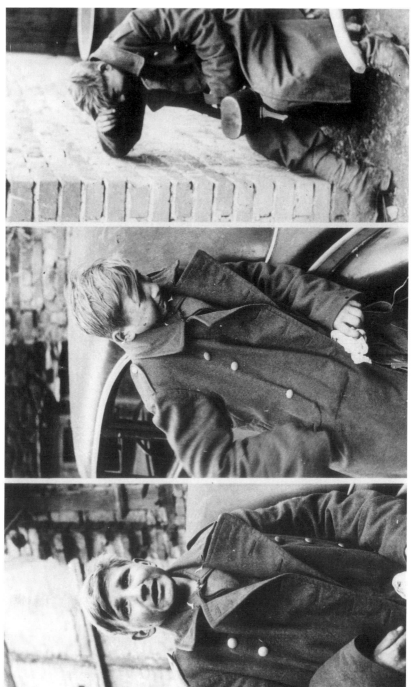

William C. Allen – AP Photo
Germany, 4 April 1945. Three faces of capture.

1

Introduction
&
Background

IN A DECADE THAT HAS SEEN both the end of the Cold War and a record number of United Nations peace-keeping and peace-building missions, tens of thousands of children and youth continue to take part in hostilities in Asia, Europe, Latin America, Africa and the Middle East. The nineties are also distinguished by fresh conflicts, largely ethnic, with new states rapidly proliferating on the international scene, and the hope that inter-state relationships can be based on the rule of law, rather than the rule of power or politics.

The 1989 United Nations Convention on the Rights of the Child reaffirms the fundamental place of the family in society, and recognizes that the child should be brought up in the spirit of the ideals in the UN Charter, in particular, peace, dignity, tolerance, freedom, and equality. The participation of children and youth in hostilities is hardly a recent phenomenon. But as we move into the twenty-first century, knowing the world's desire to protect children, must we accept as inevitable the chronic and escalating presence of armed children?

1.1 Background and Objectives

In 1991, the Swedish Red Cross, Rädda Barnen (Swedish Save the Children) and the Raoul Wallenberg Institute of Human Rights and Humanitarian Law organized a Conference on *Children of War* in Stockholm.[1] There was general agreement among the participants that the minimum age for recruitment into armed forces and for participation in conflict should be an unconditional eighteen, and that voluntary involvement of children under that age should not be permitted. Improving the rules relating to age of recruitment was identified as a long-term strategy, and it was recommended that a thorough study be undertaken of the subject of children as soldiers, in order to strengthen the ways and means of preventing their use. The present work is a direct descendant of that initiative. The Conference further recommended that the Swedish and Icelandic Red Cross Societies should propose a resolution requesting a study to the 26th International Conference of the Red Cross and the Red Crescent, then scheduled to be held in Budapest in November 1991. For various political reasons, that conference was postponed, but the proposal was duly submitted to and adopted by the Council of Delegates at its

---

1   See *Children of War*, Report from the Conference on Children of War, Stockholm, Sweden, 31 May — 2 June 1991, Raoul Wallenberg Institute, Report No. 10, Lund, 1991.

Budapest session of 28-30 November 1991.[2] In Resolution No. 14, the Council expressed its deep concern that children continue to take part in hostilities, and are recruited and sometimes encouraged or compelled to do so. It deplored the deaths and serious injury suffered by many, and the fact that others languish as prisoners of war, but it also acknowledged that children often become involved because of lack of alternative means of satisfying their basic needs of food, clothing and shelter. While noting that those under eighteen may not be sufficiently mature to understand the consequences of their actions, and to comply with international humanitarian law, the Council also recognized, in particular, that children who have participated in hostilities are often marked for life, mentally, morally and physically. The Council therefore invited States and parties to conflicts to strengthen the protection of children, for example, by way of unilateral declarations setting 18 as the minimum age for participation, and called on National Red Cross and Red Crescent Societies to do everything possible to provide basic needs and alternative activities. Specifically, the Council of Delegates requested the Henry Dunant Institute, 'to undertake a study ... on the recruitment and participation of children as soldiers in armed conflicts, and on measures to reduce and eventually eliminate such recruitment and participation.'[3]

The Henry Dunant Institute was able to initiate the present study, thanks to generous support and encouragement from the Swedish and Icelandic Red Cross Societies.[4] Building upon the 1991 Conference, the following objectives were set: to describe the nature and scope of the child soldier phenomenon (where and when it is happening and has happened in recent years) on the basis of selected first-hand field research, supplemented by secondary sources; to identify those States and non-State entities which conscript or accept the enlistment of children below the age of 18, and why they resort to under-age combatants; to identify the psychological, social, cultural, religious, material and coercive factors that lead to the participation of children in hostilities; to detail the short- and long-term consequences of participation; to set out, clearly and accessibly, the applicable rules and standards of international law and the machinery available for monitoring and ensuring compliance; to explain, as far as

2   The Council of Delegates of the International Red Cross and Red Crescent Movement is the body in which the representatives of all the components of the Movement (National Societies, International Committee of the Red Cross, International Federation of Red Cross and Red Crescent Societies) meet to discuss matters which concern the Movement as a whole. It is the executive organ of the International Red Cross movement.

3   See Resolutions adopted by the Council of Delegates, November 1991: *Int. Rev. Red Cross*, Jan.-Feb., 1992, 42, 58-9.

4   See above, Preface and Acknowledgements.

possible, the legal and cultural gaps and deficiencies in the scope and substance of the law with respect to the participation and the protection of child combatants; to identify local or national projects involving the creative and empowering use of norms and legal processes on behalf of child combatants; to develop and argue the basic principle of *non*-recruitment and *non*-participation in hostilities of any child below the age of 18; to promote acceptance of international minimum standards applicable in violent internal strife, especially as concerns participation and protection of those under age 18; to encourage ratification and respect for existing norms and improvements in national and international protection, including regional conventions, or unilateral declarations; to identify preventive alternatives to recruitment and responsive protection and rehabilitation programmes for the child soldier; to identify possible courses of action for agencies whose mandates include the responsibility to protect and assist child combatants, such as the International Committee of the Red Cross, National Red Cross and Red Crescent Societies, non-governmental organizations, and international and regional mechanisms; to signal the appropriateness of a Protocol to the Convention on the Rights of the Child; and finally, to target policy- and decision-makers with a view to promoting their adoption of the principle of non-involvement of children below the age of 18, directly or indirectly, in armed conflict.

1.2 Methodology

Although various organizations and individuals have focused considerable attention and effort on the subject of child soldiers,[5] an in-depth study of the issue, dealing also with prevention and response, has been missing. These factors dictated the approach adopted in the present work, in which we have aimed not only to see what others have said on the subject, and thus to benefit from their experience, but also to see the conditions in which children come to bear arms, thus complementing the examination of secondary sources with first-hand knowledge. We chose to concentrate on conflicts in selected countries: El Salvador, Guatemala, Israeli occupied

---

5   See in particular the regular media reviews, documentation and other material produced by Dorothea Woods of the Quaker United Nations Office, Geneva.

territories,[6] Liberia, and Sri Lanka. We felt that the situations in these countries covered nearly the full spectrum of conflict-types across a wide range of cultural, religious, and social settings. Limited time and resources prevented us from visiting many current hot-spots and we do not suggest that our empirical findings can be generalized to all conflicts. We hope that we have raised the most important issues on the recruitment and participation of child soldiers, however, and that individuals or organizations working in places we did not visit or do not mention explicitly will find the information and analysis useful and adaptable to their own contexts. In the places we did visit, Ilene Cohn had extensive meetings with children or adults involved in or affected by hostilities, and with ICRC Delegations, National Red Cross Societies, government agencies and non-governmental organizations assisting them. Most interviews were conducted confidentially, at the request of the interviewees. We also had the advantage of an interim review of objectives and progress by a Reference Group, which brought together colleagues with practical working knowledge, from within the ICRC, UNICEF, UNHCR and a variety of agencies in different parts of the world.

The convergence of information and experience from within and without confirmed for us the complexity of the issue. We see this study very much as part of a process, not an end in itself, and we hope to have made some progress in showing that something can be done to prevent children from taking up or having to take up arms, and to respond to their needs when they do become involved.

1.3   Who is the Child?

According to the 1989 United Nations Convention on the Rights of the Child, a child 'means every human being below the age of 18 years unless, under the law applicable to the child, majority is attained earlier'.[7] The possibility of a patchwork definition in international law is striking and not altogether satisfactory, as national legal systems—the applicable

---

6   We chose to include the Israeli occupied territories, and specifically the *intifada* and related violence in which children participate, rather than the occupation itself. Many of the factors which motivate youth participation and many of the consequences of participation for children and youth are similar to and pose the same sorts of challenges as those that arise in more traditional situations of armed conflict. The *intifada* does not qualify as 'hostilities' as that term is generally used in international humanitarian law, and children are not being 'recruited', as such. The situation of occupation is governed by the law, however, specifically the Fourth Geneva Convention.

7   Art. 1. The 1990 African Charter on the Rights and Welfare of the Child likewise includes every human being to the age of 18; see art. 1.

law—work their effect. The 'age of majority' is a social, religious, cultural or legal device by which societies acknowledge the transition to adulthood; and there is no *necessary* correlation between any of the levels. For the purpose of participating in religious ritual, for example, a child may become an adult at age 13.[8] For legal purposes, however, such as contracting obligations, including marriage, giving evidence under oath, being criminally liable, or voting in elections, other age requirements will prevail. On occasion, the child's actual capacity to understand will be determinative, for example, in appreciating the meaning of evidence under oath; in other cases, the legislator will make assumptions as to capacity and understanding at a certain age, for example, in setting eligibility to vote.

Although State practice displays some variation, participation in the political process is nevertheless a reasonably accurate indicator of the moment at which the community as political body recognizes the intellectual maturity of the individual. The Inter-Parliamentary Union recently reviewed the electoral systems of 150 of the world's 186 sovereign States.[9] It noted,

> The right to vote supposes that electors should have reached an age at which they are able to express an opinion on political matters, as a rule coinciding with the age of legal majority...*The norm today is eighteen years*; an overwhelming majority of 109 States has opted for this minimum age limit, with most other States having a slightly higher limit (19-21 years). The lowest limit — 16 years — is practised in four countries: Brazil, Cuba, Iran and Nicaragua.[10]

There is again no *necessary* correlation in national legislation between voting age and liability to or eligibility for military service. In Brazil, Nicaragua and Iran, the voting age is 16, but liability to military service starts at 19 in Brazil, 17 in Nicaragua, and is subject to no apparent age limit

8   This is the case in Judaism and other religions. In Islamic law, the age of majority tends to be related to puberty, though there is considerable variation in the light of cultural norms prevailing in particular communities. In a 1983 publication, *Children Bearing Military Arms,* the Quaker Office at the United Nations, Geneva, cites one Islamic scholar as pointing out that the Prophet Mohammed did not take children with him on his military expeditions; and another authority who gives examples where young males were permitted to enter battle. Criminal responsibility and puberty also go together; see Bahnassi, Ahmad Fathi, 'Criminal Responsibility in Islamic Law,' in Bassiouni, M. Cherif, ed., *The Islamic Criminal Justice System*, London, 1982, p. 192f.

9   Inter-Parliamentary Union, *Electoral Systems: A World-Wide Comparative Study*, Geneva, 1993.

10   Ibid., p. 4, (emphasis supplied). The report recognized that other factors may also enter into voter eligibility, such as residence requirements or disqualification on grounds of criminality. For voting age details, see Annex below.

in Iran.[11]

Variations also occur among States as concerns 'military age'[12], as shown in the Annex, but there is a strong tendency towards 18 or later as the minimum age for military obligations. One hundred and eighty-five States were surveyed, and among the 103 for which information was available, only seven put the age for compulsory military service below 18 years: Afghanistan, Iran, Lao People's Democratic Republic, Mexico, Namibia, Nicaragua, and South Africa; while twenty-four States permit the voluntary enlistment of young persons below 18 years of age, generally subject to parental consent: Australia, Austria, Bangladesh, Belgium, Chile, El Salvador, Finland, Germany, Greece, Guatemala, Honduras, Iran, Israel, Libya, Luxembourg, Mauritania, Netherlands, New Zealand, Norway, Poland, South Africa, United Kingdom, United States of America, and former Yugoslavia.

So far as the provisions of national laws (as opposed to actual practice) may indicate the position of States on the international law issues attaching to recruitment, a reasonable inference would support the principle of transition to adulthood at age eighteen, and the argument that young persons below that age should not be *compelled* to take up arms. The practice of requiring parental consent for voluntary enlistment below the age of eighteen is equally consistent with such a principle.

Given the essentially political dimension to armed conflict, whether national or non-international, the choice of eighteen as the moment of transition to adulthood does not seem unreasonable. Indeed, in principle, it would seem wrong to condemn the unenfranchised to die as a consequence of political decisions on which they can exercise no influence.

Moreover, international humanitarian law, international and regional human rights instruments and national legislation in numerous countries combine to proscribe the death penalty on persons under eighteen at the

---

11   At the time of writing, mid-1993, there was no conscription in Nicaragua. In a statement to the UN Human Rights Committee in 1983, the delegate for Iran is reported as saying, 'when a country is the victim of aggression, no questions were asked of volunteers joining up to defend their homeland.' *International Children's Rights Monitor*, Vol. 1, No. 2, Spring 1983, p.5. Iran's use of children, some as young as 11, in the nine-year war with Iraq, is notorious; cf. Louyot, Alain, *Les Gosses de Guerre*, Paris, 1989, pp. 22-24.

12   'Military age' is used here to signify the age at which an individual is liable to be called up (conscripted) for military service, and/or the age, usually one or two years less, at which an individual may volunteer for service, with or without parental consent. In national practice, the term 'military age' is also used to describe the whole period during which an individual may be called on to serve; for example, between the ages of 17 and 30.

time of commission of the offence.[13] This prohibition applies both in time of peace and in international and internal armed conflicts, and acknowledges the reduced ability of those under eighteen to appreciate the nature of their actions in the context of criminal responsibility. The same consideration, however, is not given to the capacity of the child or young person to evaluate the reasons for death in combat.

The idea of the child as a person under 18 thus enjoys a wide measure of support, even if different terminology, such as 'youth' or 'young persons', may be a better phrase to describe those in the crucial 15-18 age bracket, whose physical and intellectual maturity is rapidly developing even as they continue to face certain legal disabilities. If age eighteen reflects a general rule, with certain limited exceptions traceable to specific political, religious or cultural factors, the question is when and in what circumstances those under eighteen can lawfully be conscripted for military service or permitted to participate in hostilities.

1.4   Organization and Issues

This study looks first at where and in what sorts of conflicts children are fighting, and secondly, at what motivates them to take up arms or compels adults to arm children. The two issues are closely related. The dramatic changes in warfare over the past fifty years are reflected in the percentage of civilian deaths,[14] as well as in the attempts of policy-makers to develop new norms regulating the conduct of modern-day warring parties. The move to modernize international rules has been accompanied by the increased participation of children in hostilities, in terms both of numbers and of the immediate or direct nature of their involvement.[15]

---

13   Art. 68, Fourth Geneva Convention; art. 77(5), Additional Protocol I; art. 6(4), Additional Protocol II; see also art. 6(5), 1966 Covenant on Civil and Political Rights; art. 37, 1989 Convention on the Rights of the Child; art. 4(5), 1969 American Convention on Human Rights. Hereafter the four Geneva Conventions are referred to as GC1, GC2, GC3 and GC4, respectively; and the Additional Protocols as API and APII.

14   Cf. Singer, S., 'The Protection of Children during Armed Conflict Situations,' *International Review of the Red Cross*, May-June 1986, 133, 141, noting that whereas civilians counted for some 5% of casualties during World War One, that increased to some 48% during World War Two and is now even higher. Ahlström and Nordquist, *Casualties of Conflict*, Dept. of Peace and Conflict Research, Uppsala University, give 90% as that higher level of civilian casualties. See also Plattner, D., 'Protection of Children in International Humanitarian Law,' *Int. Rev. Red Cross*, 1984, 140-52.

15   For overviews of changing military tactics, combat style, army formation, civilian involvement, weapons development and other issues as they relate to the participation of children as soldiers, see Ahlström and Nordquist, *Casualties of Conflict*, (1991) pp. 6-15.

Chapter 2 tests our assumption that most young participants are neither physically forced nor coerced into joining an armed force or group, and identifies the range of reasons why a child or young person might join an armed group. We conclude that the root causes of the most prevalent types of conflict involving children and youth have much in common, and go far towards explaining their participation. An in-depth analysis of root causes is beyond the scope of this study, but they are frequently implicit or explicit in how young people explain their involvement.

The way in which conflicts are fought on the ground determines their characterization in international humanitarian law, which in turn prescribes the rules governing the conduct of hostilities. Chapter 3 looks at what international law and international humanitarian law say with regard to the regulation of different types of conflict. We aim to identify the most common characteristics of conflicts today, in order to help explain both the rise in numbers of armed children and the difficulties in using the law to prevent youth participation. Low-level internal armed conflicts and violent internal strife, which generally fall outside international humanitarian law in the strict sense, are now the most common types of conflict, and are likely to remain so in the foreseeable future. The recruitment and participation of children in these types of conflict seems to fall outside the rules. Moreover, the Convention on the Rights of the Child cannot deal directly with the recruitment and participation of children in non-state armed groups, such as opposition movements, where most youth participants are found. We examine whether existing law, even if fully implemented, would deal with the problem sufficiently, or whether new rules are called for.

Chapters 2 and 3 together show how important it is, if we really hope to reduce the numbers of child soldiers, to look beyond the fact that children do carry arms, and to understand why. In these chapters, we clarify the application of international humanitarian and human rights law to the conflicts and groups in which children fight, to highlight short-comings in legal protection, and to suggest how certain initiatives to reduce child participation or recruitment have been or might be effective.

Chapter 4 looks at the conditions in which children and youth participate in armed conflict, and at some specific consequences of their involvement. While we try to remain conscious of the wider context of each country's situation, we also focus on war's impact on child soldiers and the types of interventions that have been or might be implemented on their behalf. The evidence of negative consequences of participation will bolster the arguments against child participation, while simultaneously encouraging international and local organizations to improve their knowledge and their programmes for reducing the harmful impact of war on youth.

Chapter 5 examines the legal, programmatic and policy dimensions to responding to the consequences of children's participation in armed conflict. It reviews the legal notions of special and general protection, the responsibilities for providing protection, and the particular problem of detention. Here, we make a number of recommendations for further research and suggestions for programme planning and implementation with the aim of addressing psychosocial, physical, educational and other consequences of involvement.

Chapter 6 considers law and process at the regional and international level, and how they can be used to promote the defence of children's rights in situations of conflict.

Briefly, we review the competence and means of access to various monitoring bodies, stressing the importance of communication between local child welfare NGOs and treaty bodies on the issues of forced recruitment or participation in hostilities. We also identify some of the ways in which the protection of children and the elimination of the phenomenon of child soldiers can be promoted at the political level. Finally, we propose changes and supplements to the present law, with a view to reducing child participation.

Chapter 7 summarizes our findings and recommendations, while an annex provides tabular information on *Ratification of the Convention on the Rights of the Child, International Humanitarian Law and Human Rights Instruments, and Voting Age and Military Age by Country.*

2

The Child Soldier:
Why Children Participate in
Armed Conflict

Steve McCurry – MAGNUM
Afghanistan, 1988. School.

Gilles Peress – MAGNUM
West Belfast, Northern Ireland, 1986. Practicing.

Susan Meiselas – MAGNUM
Manila, Philippines, 1985. Poverty and structural violence, seeds of conflict.

M. Vaterlaus – ICRC
Que Son, Vietnam, 1973.

Jean Gaumy – MAGNUM
Beach at El Majagual, El Salvador, 1985. The militarization of daily life.

Larry Towell – MAGNUM
Cuidad Barrios, San Miguel, El Salvador, 1988. Forced recruitment.

Susan Meiselas – MAGNUM
Nicaragua, 1979. Martyring fallen youth.

W. Stone – UNHCR
Sudan, 1991. Boys returning.

Abbas – MAGNUM
Khajir, Nr. Khost, Afghanistan, 1986. Young militia guard at prayer.

Raymond Depardon – MAGNUM
Afghanistan, 1978. From father to son.

André Camara – AP Photo
Baghdad, Iraq 1990. Two ten-year old girls with other young members of Saddam's youth.

Raymond Depardon – MAGNUM
Beirut, Lebanon, 1978. Child snipers, proud mothers.

Jim Worrall – TREVETHICK
Northern Iraq, 1991. Young Kurd soldier.

MORE CHILDREN AND YOUTH BEAR ARMS in internal armed conflict and violent strife than ever before. Characterized by guerilla-style warfare conducted largely by part-time participants, such conflicts inevitably result in excessive civilian deaths and injuries, extensive damage to health and education systems, and substantial movements of refugees and displaced persons. When conflict drags on for years and even decades, the root causes themselves, such as poverty or repression, are exacerbated, galvanising civilian populations for recruitment into armed groups.

Any conflict leaves children and youth orphaned, displaced, or responsible as the head-of-household when one or both parents are killed or away fighting. Schools which might otherwise occupy their time are destroyed or closed, fields they might otherwise plant are off-limits because of combat or mines, relatives and neighbours are arbitrarily arrested, humiliated, abused, or tortured. Such youth are at risk for recruitment or, in their desperation, become receptive to ideological propaganda encouraging them to enlist; often a gun is a meal-ticket and a more attractive option than sitting at home afraid and helpless. Of course, youth have trained for battle throughout history, but the weight of the weapons often limited their actual involvement. Today, arms technology is so advanced that even small boys and girls can handle common weapons like M16 and AK47 assault rifles. More children can be more useful in battle with less training than ever before, putting them in more danger and making them more dangerous to their adversaries—a factor that makes them attractive as recruits.

Instances in which children and youth are or have been coerced into joining government armed forces, for example, in Burma, Guatemala, El Salvador, and Ethiopia, or opposition movements, as in Mozambique, Angola, Sri Lanka, Sudan, are obvious examples of victimization. But children and youth are not necessarily driven into conflict. Sometimes, as in Liberia, they are among the first to join armed groups; at other times, as in the Palestinian *intifada* in the Israeli occupied territories, they are primary catalysts of violent strife. Their motivation lies in the very roots of the conflicts, in the predominant macro social, economic and political issues defining their lives. Overwhelming as it may seem, confronting these larger concerns may be the only realistic road to preventing youth participation in otherwise unavoidable hostilities.

This chapter charts the ways in which children come to participate in armed forces and groups, beginning with forced and coerced recruitment and moving to voluntary participation. We explore a range of reasons offered by children and youth to explain their participation. A very fuzzy line is often all that separates voluntary from coerced participation, and it is impossible to know precisely at what age or developmental stage a young person is capable of 'volunteering' in the way we would accept of an adult. No one makes a decision in a vacuum, but clearly a child may be particularly susceptible to certain types of pressure coming from certain people.

2.1 Recruitment of Children and Youth into Armed Forces and/or Groups

2.1.1 Forced recruitment

Forced recruitment, entailing the threat or actual violation of the physical integrity of the youth or someone close to him or her, is practised by both armed opposition groups and national armed forces. Even some States in which conscription is regulated by law engage in systematic forced recruitment, sweeping up under-age adolescents along with young men.

In El Salvador through 1991 and until today in Guatemala, the armed forces use round-ups to fill the ranks, taking young men out of buses and cars, away from market-places or churches or as they walk down the road. Neither country maintains a formal conscription process, so prevention is not just a question of making sure that citizens know their rights. Many peasants have no identification cards documenting their date of birth, because the birth was not formally registered, or the registry has been destroyed in the fighting, or because identification cards are not issued until their eighteenth birthday. Those swept up in recruitment drives, if anyone ever listens to them, often have difficulty proving they are under age or that they fall within exempted categories, such as students or only sons.

New recruits are moved from training centres to posts far from home. Families are not always notified, and locating the son or husband can be time-consuming and expensive for a peasant family. Verbal protests outside a training centre or army barracks inevitably prove futile, and if they can finally produce the necessary papers and hand them over to the right official, they risk losing them without gaining the release of the recruit. Both legal assistance and bribes and 'fines' are beyond reach in most cases; and families of recruits told us that as the recruit moves deeper into the system, so the officials become more reluctant to release him.

Shortages of manpower and *class discrimination* explain much of the forced recruitment by the Salvadoran armed forces up until 1992. Legislation for systematic and fair conscription was never considered 'necessary' throughout the entire civil war. Army salaries rarely lured even the poor to enlist, especially with the high casualty rate on the front lines. Young men from the wealthier families were neither suspected of communist tendencies, nor found riding the country buses that were targeted for recruitment sweeps, while those with cash in hand could pay an unofficial 'fine' in exchange for a son or brother. The civilian-participant line was also very blurred and officials may have hoped that recruiting from certain villages in areas of possible guerilla support ensured a measure of population control. Soldier morale appears to have been of far less importance to the army than to the opposition *Farabundo Marti National Liberation Front (FMLN)*.

Forced recruitment by the FMLN, including under-15s, was reported between 1980 and 1986. Persons displaced from towns in the north east of the country claimed that if they had stayed home, children between the ages of 6 and 12 would have been required to go to the guerrillas' school; children between the ages of 12 and 15 would have undergone military training; and those between 16 and 40 would have been required to perform military service. Although many Salvadorans fled to escape the forced recruitment of their children, others also fled the government, fearing to be regarded as legitimate targets if they chose to remain in guerilla-controlled territory in which no one was considered neutral.[1]

The Center on War and the Child, an Arkansas-based NGO, reported that in 1983 one of five parties forming the FMLN had warned residents of one community in a combat zone that any young man who did not join them should leave town. Some who did neither were killed, but forced recruitment by the guerrillas was abandoned in 1986, because it led to loss of political support. A guerilla leader speaking to journalists in 1987 explained the change of policy by the FMLN: 'We don't need cannon fodder, we need consciousness, and without that, it's better that they stay home.'[2]

Population control also explains the recruitment into the paramilitary civil defence patrols (PACs) of indigenous Mayan villagers in Guatemala, including some as young as fourteen. Although article 34 of the Guatemalan Constitution clearly describes the PACs as voluntary organizations, army officials justify their actions to villagers by arguing that as the PAC system is organized in defence of democracy, a refusal to participate reveals anti-democratic sentiments and the resister 'must be' an enemy communist guerilla. In reality, the average Guatemalan campesino knows that civil

---

1   *Free Fire: A Report on Human Rights in El Salvador*, Americas Watch and Lawyers Committee for International Human Rights, (Aug. 1984, Fifth Supplement), pp.54-6.

2   'Youth Under Fire: Military Conscription in El Salvador,' Center on War and the Child, Arkansas, 1989.

patrols rarely confront the guerilla. Participating in the PAC costs a day each week or so, which would otherwise be spent employed or subsistence farming, but dismissal from PAC duty would cost a 'fine' higher than a day's wage, and outright refusal could be costly indeed.[3]

Ethiopian youth, forcibly recruited because of lack of manpower in the Mengistu government's fight against separatist Eritreans, were denounced by their own commanders as deserters once captured by the opposition. An estimated 14,000-20,000 Ethiopian government troops were captured over the years by the *Eritrean Peoples Liberation Front (*EPLF*)*, with at least several hundred estimated to be at most 14 years old.[4]

All adult males (from age 20) are legally eligible for conscription into the Mozambican Armed Forces (FAM), yet when confronted with manpower shortages and little response to the compulsory military service campaigns, standard recruitment procedures have been combined with forcible conscription at gunpoint.[5] According to Africa Watch, frequent mass desertions mitigate the effectiveness of forced recruitment, which is neither publicly nor institutionally sanctioned.

The Mozambican resistance (RENAMO) consistently and systematically practised forced recruitment, and evidence suggests that children are preferred to adult combatants. A RENAMO deserter forcibly recruited at age ten explained that 'RENAMO does not use many adults to fight because they are not good fighters...kids have more stamina, are better at surviving in the bush, do not complain, and follow directions.'[6] Much larger numbers of very young soldiers (as young as six, seven and eight years old) have been recruited since the late 1980s. One commentator has described child combatants as undisciplined and sometimes on drugs; they appear to have undergone trauma and deprivation, and to have been programmed to feel little fear or revulsion for the massacres which they carry out with greater enthusiasm and brutality than adults.[7]

3   Many CERJ members have been threatened, disappeared or killed for resisting forced participation in the PACs; see *Persecution by Proxy: The Civil Patrols in Guatemala*, The Robert F. Kennedy Memorial Center for Human Rights, New York, 1993.

4   T. Lansner, 'Dragged from Soccer Fields to Killing Fields,' *Sydney Morning Herald*, 11 Jun. 1988, p.29. Numbers and ages are impossible to verify since the EPLF denied the International Committee of the Red Cross (ICRC) access to detainees.

5   *Conspicuous Destruction: War, Famine and the Reform Process in Mozambique*, Africa Watch, July 1992, p.4.

6   US Defense Intelligence Agency, Report on RENAMO deserter, March 1991, quoted in *Conspicuous Destruction: War, Famine & the Reform Process in Mozambique*, above note 7, at 96-7. See also *The Children of Mozambique's Killing Fields*, Center on War and the Child, Eureka Springs, 1989, quoting a RENAMO military adviser to the effect that there was a systematic preference for children, because it was easier to keep them from running away than to control adults.

7   Alex Vines, *RENAMO: Terrorism in Mozambique*, London, 1991, pp.95-6. Much the same is being said of Liberian child soldiers today.

One veteran observer of children in war described the following scene, which typifies the plight of hundreds of Mozambican children:

When RENAMO...abducted Alfredo, they tied his hands behind his back, put a 50 kilo bag of stolen food on his head, and forced him to march like that for two days to the RENAMO base camp....'The bandits killed my mother, And my brothers too. They took me to their base camp. Yes, I was with the bandits. I had a gun. The chief taught me to use it. He beat me up. I had a gun to kill. I killed people and soldiers. I didn't like it. I killed. I killed.'[8]

Young, impressionable children can be turned into the fiercest fighters through brutal indoctrination. A typical RENAMO recruitment practice involved taking a boy soldier back to his village and forcing him to kill someone known to him. 'The killing took place in such a way that the community knew that he had killed, thus effectively closing the door to the child ever returning to his village.'[9] Such children may develop a dependency relationship with their captors, eventually even coming to identify with their cause.[10]

Some RENAMO soldiers volunteered for duty, usually after injustice at the hands of government troops; others were forcibly recruited and gradually converted to supporters; still others were taken from zones where local chiefs support the movement. A significant number, however, were picked up at random in the countryside or in raids, marched to base camps, put through training and threatened with beatings or death should they attempt to desert. Recruitment of children increased rather than abated over the years and was heaviest in areas from which adult men had migrated for work and in other places where local support for RENAMO was low.

In Peru, both the military and the guerrilla forces forcibly recruit youth. In an effort to mobilize peasants against *Sendero Luminoso* and to control residents' movements, the military employs a system of civil patrols which, like in Guatemala, replaces traditional leadership structures and ignores traditional values.

The patrols comprise women and very young people, barely teenagers, as well as men. No one is paid, and there is no provision for reparation or

---

8   Neil Boothby, 'Living in the War Zone,' in US Committee for Refugees, *World Refugee Survey - 1989 in Review*, pp. 40-1.

9   Cole P. Dodge, Magne Raundalen, *Reaching Children in War: Sudan, Uganda and Mozambique* Sigma Forlut, Norway (1991) p.57.

10   Ibid.

care in the case of wounding or a family's loss of a parent. In some cases, particularly in Ayacucho during the past two years, Sendero's brutality has provoked some villages to form patrols voluntarily; but the bulk...are created through pressure from the army and navy...Villages with patrols are favored targets of Sendero; it is not uncommon for large groups of villagers to be murdered because they participate in a civil patrol....the peasants are first pressed into patrol service, then left for Sendero reprisals.[11]

Peasant leaders have denounced the compulsory nature of the civil patrols, preferring agrarian reform over militarization as a way to improve life in the countryside. In fact, patrols have contributed to an escalation in violence, both by and against patrollers.[12]

Statistics on forced recruitment by Sendero Luminoso are unavailable. Human rights monitors have reported that youth are forced to participate in training exercises in remote guerrilla camps, where they also undergo indoctrination. Relief workers have received many requests from those who have escaped and want to leave the country.[13]

2.1.2 Coercive or abusive recruitment

Coercive or abusive recruitment covers those situations where there is no proof of direct physical threat or intimidation, but the evidence supports the inference of involuntary enlistment. The prohibitions on recruiting children in international human rights or humanitarian law apply to any and all recruitment: forced, coerced or voluntary. The present distinctions help to explain the motivation of the recruiters and/or the children, in the belief that therein lies part of the answer to why existing law fails to eliminate the recruitment of children and youth.

Between the late-1980s and 1992 some 12,500 Sudanese boys wandered across two thousand kilometres of desert between Sudan, Ethiopia and Kenya. It was speculated that they had been removed from their families at a very young age by Sudanese rebel forces, the *Sudanese Peoples Liberation Army* (SPLA), trying to ensure a future supply of fighters. The criterion for selection into this children's militia was said by some reporters to be the presence of two molar teeth. Other reports said that the

---

11   'Into the Quagmire: Human Rights and U.S. Policy in Peru', Americas Watch, Sept. 1991, p.14.
12   Ibid.
13   Coletta Youngers, 'Peru Under Scrutiny: Human Rights and U.S. Drug Policy', WOLA Briefing Series: Issues in International Drug Policy, Washington D.C., 13 Jan. 1992, p.14.

boys had been used as advance troops, to clear minefields.[14] The Office of the United Nations High Commissioner for Refugees (UNHCR) indicated that once they arrived in Ethiopia with their teachers (some of whom were SPLA members) in the mid-1980s, many of them received paramilitary training.[15] When the Ethiopian government fell in May 1991, they travelled back to southern Sudan where the International Committee of the Red Cross (ICRC) reported no evidence of the boys' military conscription. In February 1992 the group moved on to refugee camps in Kenya. Although reported to have 'no sense of national identity' and to want to be reunited with their families, they seemed to many to 'have become their own substitute family, providing a sense of security and belonging.'[16]

An international civil servant previously stationed in Burma (Myanmar), reports that the Karens and other ethnic groups as well as the Burmese army all recruit children. Those left in orphanages by families too poor to care for them, and street children denounced as 'vagrants' and placed in institutions, also often end up in the military.[17]

Although the conflict between Sri Lankan Tamils and Sinhalese can be traced back to the 1950s, and serious combat to 1983, it was only with the intervention of the Indian Peace-Keeping Forces in 1987 that the Liberation Tigers of Tamil Eelam (LTTE) faced a manpower shortage, leading to the recruitment of boys as young as 9 to 12 years old. Recruitment of young boys increased again in 1990 when conflict erupted for the second time. Enlistment is supposedly 'voluntary', meaning that no one is physically threatened. But some families were reportedly menaced with property confiscation or physical violence if they appeared unwilling to contribute their sons to the cause.[18]

Silesian Brothers working in areas controlled by Charles Taylor's National Patriotic Front of Liberia (NPFL) in October 1992 reported forced recruitment at schools run by the church. It was unclear whether Taylor required local commanders to fill quotas with new recruits, or whether this was a spontaneous initiative by local field commanders.

---

14 P. Moumtzis, 'Children of War,' *Refugees*, UNHCR Quarterly Report, July 1992, pp. 30-2.
15 Ibid.
16 Ibid.
17 Confidential interview conducted by Ilene Cohn.
18 Information gathered during field mission; sources requested anonymity.

2.2   Why Children and Youth join Armed Forces or Groups

The vast majority of young soldiers are not forced or coerced into participating in conflict, but are subject to many subtly manipulative motivations and pressures that are all the more difficult to eliminate than blatant forced recruitment. A composite picture of the child soldier in a given conflict might help our understanding of why some children fight, but broad generalizations are difficult in the case of voluntary participation, because the motivating factors are so varied. In interviews, urban, upper middle class Salvadorans who volunteered for the FMLN at young ages gave reasons quite distinct from those of young, poorer, rural Salvadoran FMLN combatants. Each situation and each perspective varies, but knowing who is the child soldier in a given conflict is a good starting point for anyone hoping to reduce volunteerism.

Children differ widely, both within and across areas of armed conflict, in the nature of their pre-war and war-related experiences. Several studies have explored the extent to which the objective features of children's war-related experiences and children's subjective appraisals, or comprehension, of their experiences are the basis for negative or positive psychosocial outcomes.[19] Anecdotal evidence supports the supposition that many young people voluntarily join armed groups or forces because of their personal experiences and circumstances, and in light of their subjective appraisal of the decision to volunteer.

Children's subjective understanding of reality is influenced by their social milieu or what has come to be called children's ecologies, and by developmental processes. The ecologies of children's lives—their parents, families, peer groups, schools, religious communities and other community-based institutions—might exert pressures or send messages that lead children to participate in hostilities. Members of children's ecologies may also influence how a youth appraises the choice to participate in hostilities or not.

Developmental processes, or stages children pass through at different ages, that influence a child's understanding of objective experiences can induce a child to respond to circumstances by joining an armed group. Developmental stage will also affect a child's perception of the decision to join. Children's expectations and feelings of empowerment and competence, both before and during war, have an impact on their decision

19   Mona Macksoud and J. Lawrence Aber, 'The War Experiences and Psychosocial Development of Children in Lebanon', *Child Development* (in press); Jose Luis Henriquez y Milagros Mendez, 'Los Efectos Psicosociales de la Guerra en Niños de El Salvador', *Revista de Psicología de El Salvador*, vol.XI, no.44, San Salvador (1992).

to take up arms. Differences in children's 'attributional styles' are equally at work. For example, those who spontaneously attribute the cause of negative events to external factors might be more likely to seek revenge. As adolescents enter the identity formation stage, the meaning they attach to the roles that conflict offers, such as combatant, victim, hero, or leader, may influence their decision to join an armed group. At this developmental stage, the ability to project a meaningful future for themselves is also powerfully and intimately tied up with their role in the conflict.

This framework for examining why some youth voluntarily join armed groups offers at least three areas for intervention, with a view to reducing volunteerism: first, interventions aimed at structural reform (improving or eliminating the structural causes of profoundly negative personal experiences); secondly, interventions aimed at youth's appraisals of participation as a means of affecting change; and thirdly, interventions that counter children's feelings of helplessness, vulnerability and frustration.

2.2.1 Objective features of children's pre-war and war-related experiences

2.2.1.1 Militarization of daily life

Militarization includes heavily armed policemen or soldiers patrolling the streets, military personnel occupying high government posts, military censorship of social life, armed guards in schools and public buildings, armed checkpoints along the roads, and curfews. Militarization is a factor in the everyday lives of many children, even before or aside from actual conflict. El Salvador in the late 1970s and 1980s was one example, the rural highlands of Guatemala and the townships of South Africa are others. The Sri Lankan LTTE has been known to broadcast Rambo-like TV movies of live combat training and actual combat, parade young soldier units before school children as they emerge from classes, conduct military training inside school grounds, and give talks at schools about the need for soldiers to man all the guns they have. At least one school in the LTTE zone has a combination memorial hall and playground, full of photos of young martyrs and a play area with toy guns mounted on the see-saws. Tamil children spend one or two hours per day out of school digging bunkers, a form of 'militarized civic duty' and are eventually asked to join the LTTE. The LTTE's militarization of education in northern Sri Lanka increased in 1987, when manpower was short and combat frequent.

With declining state investment in the educational system, about sixty percent of Peru's 7.7 million schoolchildren live in zones where the *Sendero*

Luminoso exerts limited to extensive control over the schools. In areas under guerilla control curricula include, 'mathematics, military-style calesthenics, and "labor education" — the sewing of uniforms, bandages and backpacks.' Journalists report that classes are interrupted for 'popular assemblies', students are recruited, certain courses are prohibited and 'bad teachers' are punished.[20]

Refugee camps can also be highly militarized environments, often exposed to attack, where refugee children are vulnerable to political exploitation.[21] '... under the umbrella of 'humanitarian aid,' not only are guns being delivered to refugees in many parts of the world, but under-aged children are being primed to use them.'[22] As recently as August 1992, some two thousand unaccompanied Sudanese refugee children went missing from a transit camp in Kenya and are presumed to have joined, or been recruited by, the SPLA in southern Sudan.

2.2.1.2 *Physical and/or structural violence*[23]

Many children who later choose to become soldiers have personally experienced or witnessed extremes of physical violence, including summary executions, death squad killings, disappearances, torture, arbitrary arrest or detention, sexual abuse, bombings, forced displacement, destruction of home or property, and massacres. Such experiences often produce the desire for revenge, the conviction to continue the struggles of lost loved ones, the need to substitute an annihilated family or social structure, and the desire to take control over events that shape one's circumstances. We interviewed a Salvadoran young man who had attempted unsuccessfully to enlist in the army four times, hoping for a paying job. He joined the FMLN only after being arrested by the army, charged with subversion, tortured and released. 'I had never known how brutal soldiers could be and I had heard lots of FMLN talks about fighting for the poor, so the next time they passed through my town I went with them.'

Social and economic injustice motivates adults and children to take up arms, sometimes with a long-term vision of effecting change, and at other

20   James Brooke, 'Shining Path Rebels Infiltrate Peru's Schools,' *New York Times*, 30 Aug. 1992 at 8.

21   See below, on measures to protect the civilian character of refugee camps and to maintain their immunity from armed attack.

22   Neil Boothby and John Humphrey, 'Under the Gun - Children in Exile', V. Hamilton, ed., U.S. Committee for Refugees, Wash. D.C., 1988.

23   Structural violence, is 'violence committed on behalf of or with the support of a social structure, such as apartheid or systematic discrimination against a minority.' Everett M. Ressler, *Children in War: A Guide to the Provision of Services*, UNICEF, New Yor, 1993, p.20.

times just to get food for the day. Some young people assume the risk of voluntary participation to obtain a subsistence wage. When survival is the major motivation, combatants are unlikely to abandon their arms until they see that those needs are being met. UNICEF Sri Lanka reported that 'wide disparities in socio-economic status, employment opportunities, and access to welfare services' contributed to ethnic tensions resulting in the outbreak of violence in the 1980s. That conflict in turn diverted funds away from welfare and social services to defence and internal security,[24] generating a vicious circle in which, paradoxically, arms alone appear to ensure the best chance of survival. Filipino child care workers have documented the same route to becoming a child soldier: social injustice, poverty, insurrection, increasingly unavailable basic services, increased volunteerism among youth.[25]

By the time Liberia's civil war reached the capital in 1990, the director of the Liberian Red Cross had witnessed 7-year-olds in combat because, he believes, 'those with guns could eat', and the promise of loot was irresistible. The same is undoubtedly as true for many of the estimated 8,000 Mozambican child 'bandidos', as it is for many children in Burma and Sri Lanka.

Before the end of the Cold War and the prevalence of ethnic conflicts, governments' disregard for the welfare of citizens and failure to curb violent abuses of fundamental rights were common justifications for civil conflicts.[26]

2.2.1.3 The better of the bad alternatives

For refugees, the internally displaced, the homeless, the orphaned, and the fearful, joining an armed group sometimes appears the better of the bad alternatives. The limits of life in a refugee camp can make an armed group appear very attractive to restless youth. Commenting on the decision of a 14-year old Guatemalan refugee boy in Mexico to cross the border and join the insurgency, one psychologist noted that:

> even younger children in less hostile worlds are capable of what psychologists refer to as intuitive political thinking, not only showing

24   *A Profile of the Sri Lankan Child in Crisis and Conflict*, UNICEF Colombo (1990) at 1.

25   Elizabeth Marcelino, 'Children at War', *Children of the Storm*, Official publication of the Children's Rehabilitation Center, Manila, July 1991-March 1992, at 3. After questioning Khmer refugees at the Thai border, Neil Boothby concluded that lack of food and protection led many Cambodian children to join armed groups between 1979-89; see 'Children and War,' 10 *Cultural Survival Quarterly*, No. 4 (1986).

26   Everett M. Ressler, *Children in War: A Guide to the Provision of Services*, above note 23, at 20.

evidence of socialization, but of idiosyncratic yet imaginative political opinions as well. Through their endless series of why questions, children as young as three-year-olds begin to make rudimentary inquiries into social inequities they spot outside the home, and in doing so, can challenge their own parents' complacent ways. This innate curiosity of children is heightened when they are uprooted from their homes and communities. Everyday struggles for food, shelter and other basic necessities can make their need to comprehend — and, at times, to act, even more pressing.[27]

Inadequate education and other facilities for the Sri Lankan repatriates in displaced persons camps can make the LTTE seem like a viable option.[28] It may be disagreeable but it is a known entity, whereas the army is the unknown, feared alternative.

Uganda's National Resistance Army (NRA), which took power in January 1986 after the overthrow of President Obote, contained an estimated 3,000 children under 16, including 500 girls. Child soldiers, described as disciplined, reliable and trustworthy, were highly visible among the 'liberating forces'.[29] Most had been orphaned during the Obote army's rampages through the countryside, which left an estimated 200,000 persons killed over four and half years. 'These children were taken in by the army when their parents died,' an official said. 'They looked to the army and now the state, as surrogates, as parents.'[30] But that substitute family was often secondary to the fact that they had personally lived through the massacre of their own family, friends, and community, in an experience beyond remedy and certain to influence the rest of their lives. Many Salvadoran children suffered in the same way, and for them too the FMLN provided a close-knit social structure.

In countries like Guatemala or El Salvador until 1992, joining the opposition often seemed more attractive than being forcibly and arbitrarily recruited by the army. According to peasant leaders interviewed in Guatemala: 'the guerrilla don't force anyone to kill people, except in combat', 'the food in the army barracks is not the traditional peasant beans and tortillas', 'military training involves lots of beatings and conditioning that destroys indigenous culture and values', 'people can at least imagine

27 Neil Boothby and John Humphrey, above note 22.
28 UNHCR Colombo claims there is no LTTE recruitment going on in the repatriate camps in government-controlled areas.
29 Cole P. Dodge, Magne Raundalen, *Reaching Children in War: Sudan, Uganda and Mozambique* above note 9, at 54-5.
30 E. Gargan, 'In Uganda, a Children's Army,' *Int'l. Herald Tribune*, 5 Aug. 86; also Michelle Chandler, 'Uganda's Child Warriors,' *African Concord*, 17 Apr. 1986.

that the guerrillas fight for the good of the people' and 'a volunteer can leave any time he wants.' We interviewed a 16-year-old ex-FMLN-combatant who had joined at age 13. His brother had joined years earlier but this boy's deciding moment came when he escaped forced recruitment into the army. 'I know that once the army recruits you, you are kept in by force, you need permission to visit your family and permission is rarely given. It's better to join a voluntary organization, where permission to visit your family is at least possible.' The FMLN also provided a social support structure, validation, discipline, respect and protection to many kids who had witnessed family members or teachers killed or ill-treated, or whose families lived in Honduran refugee camps. The clothes, basic medical attention and food provided to young fighters were rare commodities in many homes.

2.2.2 Subjective appraisals: a child's evolving capacity to evaluate and to decide[31]

How children or young adults perceive and explain their personal experiences influences their decision to join one or another armed group. Adults, whether parents or military officers, may well have explanations that differ greatly from how the young soldier explains his or her decision. For example, leaders and devotees of armed opposition groups, like Liberia's NPFL, the Afghan Mujahedin or El Salvador's FMLN, often deny they could prevent zealous children from joining voluntarily in support of 'the cause'. The Sri Lankan LTTE claims its young recruits are 'volunteers for the cause' and it would be unthinkable to 'refuse their desire to combat Sinhalese imperialism, which is the concern of all Tamils.'

Some children or youth do profess loyalty to a religious, nationalistic, or political ideology in the name of which they take up arms. But examples of youth indoctrination leading to enlistment negate any presumption of 'voluntary participation for the cause'. Instead they suggest that youth may not have the cognitive capacity to think rationally about concepts like ideology and nation. Some Sri Lankans felt their children were attracted by the black and white vision of the world offered by the LTTE, which presents itself as sacred and infallible. The same may be true for many youth enticed to join the Iranian army in the 1980s. A Palestinian journalist credits activist youth with 'a good command of the basics of politics', by which he means understanding things in terms of black and white, good and bad, friend and

---

31   Article 12 of the Convention on the Rights of the Child mandates that children who are capable of forming their own views shall have the right to express those views freely in all matters affecting them, 'the views of the child being given due weight in accordance with the age and maturity of the child.'

enemy.[32] Because no science has established an age at which all young people are capable of balancing commitment to beliefs against physical risk, it is instructive to hear why children take up arms, as understood by the range of those involved: the children themselves, their families, peers, teachers, communities, and military leaders.

Some explanations from the field lead us to doubt the evaluative capacities of some young fighters, at least with regard to a decision that potentially has such serious consequences. A Palestinian defence attorney claims her young clients throw stones to 'prove' they are not collaborators with the Israeli Defence Forces. A journalist who interviewed Liberian boy soldiers at NPFL checkpoints, reported that they believed fantastic promises of future rewards, as did more than one Sri Lankan Tamil boy who ran away from home to join the LTTE believing he would learn to ride a tractor or a motorcycle, or would get special glasses for motorcycle riding. The promise of adventure must be understood against the child's personal circumstances, as refugee, street child, orphan, victim or witness to violence. Recruiters for Liberia's armed forces (AFL) were reportedly overwhelmed in January 1990 with volunteer street children who, according to one witness, 'wanted to get up to Nimba County and *do* something for their country; they felt it would be more interesting than street life.' A Liberian human rights worker is convinced that the bulk of the 9-10 year olds in the NPFL's Small Boy Units, joined for the Rambo-esque 'adventure' of it.

Such explanations, by raising the question of children's evolving capacities to determine what is in their best interests, cast doubt on the argument that children are capable of exercising their right of free association or freedom of movement by joining an armed group.[33] In asking why youth volunteer for combat, we often learn that they are highly influenced by community and peer groups, or by factors they have little capacity to analyze. And, as with many adult combatants, we learn that in many cases, were fundamental rights respected in the first place, the armed alternative would be unnecessary. The proliferation of ethnic conflicts fuelled by the generational transmission of adult hatreds makes it increasingly important to focus on the influence of adults' subjective perceptions on children.

---

32   David Kuttab, 'A Profile of the Stonethrowers', 17 *J. of Palestine Studies* 14, 18 (Spring 1988).
33   *Children of War*, Report from the Conference on Children of War, Raoul Wallenberg Institute, Swedish Red Cross, Swedish Save the Children, 1991, pp.39-40.

2.2.3 The influence of children's ecologies

2.2.3.1 Religion, ideology and indoctrination

In 1986, Human Rights Watch (HRW) described the war being waged by the Soviet occupying forces and the Mujahedin resistance fighters for the allegiance of Afghan children. Thousands were being sent to the Soviet Union for long-term indoctrination or training as spies, saboteurs and assassins. A resistance commander explained: '[The Soviets] saw that they couldn't conquer us and they realized that there was no way to change the people. That's when they decided to take the children, because they think that they have "empty brains".'[34]

The Mujahedin also concentrated on 'arming their children spiritually and emotionally for the battles that lie ahead.'[35] The director of an orphanage in Pakistan insisted that: '[t]he fighting in Afghanistan is for an ideology, for a cause. The Russians are imposing their ideology. But we have our own. We have plans to see that our ideology is not defeated.'[36] In Pakistan, that plan centred partly on the indoctrination of the 48% of the 5 million refugees who were children. Asked about his future plans, one seven-year-old orphan said that he would line up all the mujahedin and will lead them to avenge the death of his father. 'We will attack the Russians and kill all of them.' The adults in the room smiled appreciatively and proudly at his answer.[37] Military leaders and parents in refugee camps are often anxious that their children not forget or abandon the homeland, they 'feel the need to bring their children more fully (and more quickly) into their political struggles', even if it means risking their lives.[38]

In early 1988 a New York Times reporter interviewed Iranian POW children in Iraq, who had been recruited by the Iranian armed forces in ways and for reasons closely resembling those of the Mujahedin. 'A score of interviews, in which catch phrases seemed to recur, suggested that recruiting drives were pursued in schools, on the radio and in the streets in towns and cities across Iran. According to these accounts, young men flocked to recruitment centres, fired by the depiction of the Iraqis as unbelievers bereft of divine protection. They were given assault rifles and a little training, shipped to an indistinct front and ordered to charge a foe superior in armaments.'[39]

---

34 *To Win the Children: Afghanistan's Other War*, Helsinki Watch/Asia Watch (1986), p.2.
35 Ibid.
36 Ibid., at 15.
37 Ibid., at 14.
38 Neil Boothby and John Humphrey, above note 22.
39 A. Cowell, 'For Prisoners of War: Boys' Camp?' *New York Times*, 17 Feb. 1988, A4, cols. 5-6.

The Center on War and the Child confirmed the accounts of Iranian children propelled into combat with minimal training, but adequately armed with 'headbands with religious slogans and khaki jackets bearing the message that they have "permission" of the imam to enter heaven, along with keys on chains around their necks ensuring such entry.'[40]

When an Afghan child spy trained by the Russians was captured by the Mujahedin he was 'rehabilitated' or brought 'back to Islam', and sent back to Kabul as a Mujahedin spy. It was not the forced participation of their children that the Mujahedin resented; what mattered was whose ideology their participation advanced.[41] Even resistance commanders who may not have approved of training children as spies or assassins seemed to feel that the cause warranted the use of all available resources.[42]

We cannot know to what extent young combatants in these two wars truly understood or freely associated themselves with one or another ideology. An Iranian POW in Iraq, asked whether at 14 years-old he had really wanted to be a hero, let alone a martyr, replied as if repeating tutored lines that, 'his recruitment as a volunteer in Iranian forces fighting Iraq was a deception.' Another prisoner recalled his last charge on the southern front of the Iran-Iraq war, when he was 15 years-old: 'They told us to shout "God is great!"...We were told that because we were believers we would win. But we saw the opposite thing.' His Iraqi captors nodded and smiled their approval.[43]

It is impossible to know how children might express themselves when not under the watchful eyes of their teachers, caretakers, or captors. But it is equally difficult to imagine how Iranian or Afghan children might have been prevented from engaging in combat, when their participation was so highly valued by the adults most prominent in their lives. Again and again we hear children reciting the hateful, violent, or resentful lines that are sure to win the approval of those they love or those in charge. This parroting of values denies the validity of any attempt to cast the participation of these child soldiers as truly voluntary. The context confirms, however, that an effective policy against youth recruitment will have to take account of adult perceptions and values.

2.2.3.2 Social, community and family values

Social, community and family values influence children's appraisals of their circumstances and their assessment of the decision whether or not to

---

40   J. Hughes, 'Children at War,' *Christian Science Monitor*, 28 Oct. 1987.
41   *To Win the Children: Afghanistan's Other War*, above note 34, at 19-20.
42   Ibid. at 20.
43   A. Cowell, 'For Prisoners of War: Boys' Camp?' *New York Times*, above note 39.

participate in hostilities. How communities 'value' the reasons for conflict, for example, in terms of social justice, religious fanaticism, ethnic purity, redress of historic wrongs, is likely to be central to children's own perceptions. If intra-familial and community violence are prevalent, this may override rational decision-making processes or non-violent options for conflict resolution. Children may perceive a violent response to the structural or political problems as the 'only' choice. A Salvadoran psychologist suggested that excessive militarization of a society leads to a 'mental militarization', in which violent response to social problems is the norm.[44]

Children can also pick up 'mixed messages' from adults. Some Palestinian parents in the Israeli occupied territories are proud of their activist children, even as they fear for their safety. Some Sri Lankan Tamil families support the LTTE, while going to great lengths to prevent their own children from joining. Before 1990, when the LTTE retained a larger measure of popular support in the north, they were respected for their strict discipline, including a ban on alcohol, and for their 'fairness', for example, in demanding money only from those who could afford it. Children understood that the community valued these qualities, which may in turn have influenced their joining the LTTE rather than another armed Tamil group.[45]

How a society or armed group refers to its dead can also be a source of pressure. Sri Lankan LTTE dead are referred to as martyrs in northern Jaffna, and their families are well looked after, being provided with free food and transport to and from Jaffna. Similar martyring of the dead occurs in the Philippines, among NPA supporters, in the Israeli occupied territories, and was a powerful influence in Iran during the war with Iraq.

Given the extent to which children's perceptions of family and community values influence decisions to join the military or an armed group, interventions to reduce volunteerism must be directed as much at children's ecologies as at the children themselves. In some cases, evidence of the serious consequences of participation for child soldiers, their families and communities, might help reduce the short-term pride in participation.[46] In other cases, however, immediate survival needs or the long-term macro objectives of adults may outweigh concerns for child participants. For example, after 1987 any Sri Lankan family with the means moved south, emigrated, or sent their children out of Jaffna. Now, those between 15 and

---

44   Ignacio Martín-Baró, 'La Violencia Política y la Guerra como Causas del Trauma Psicosocial en El Salvador', *Revista de Psicología de El Salvador* vol. VII, no. 28, 123-41, 1988.

45   Information from the field; names withheld at interviewees' request.

46   See Chapter 3, below.

35 years old are prohibited from leaving the whole of the northern zone where the LTTE exercises authority, it can cost 300,000 Rupees (approx. US$7000) to buy an exit pass, and the poorer families remain trapped. In such circumstances, it can be hard to convince people to overlook their own and their children's immediate survival needs, if these can only be satisfied by joining the LTTE. Alternatively, if an entire community or group perceives a risk to its own survival, validation or acceptance of the participation of their children in the struggle will be difficult to resist.

2.2.3.3 Peer pressure

Peer pressure can be as persuasive as a child's desire to win the approval of family or religious leaders. For many young Palestinians, '[t]o throw a stone is to be "one of the guys"; to hit an Israeli car is to become a hero; and to be arrested and not confess to having done anything is to be a man.'[47] According to a West Bank psychologist, ideology is the last thing her injured young clients cite as a motivation, after peer pressure and the desire for revenge. In Liberia too the feeling that 'everyone is doing it' is a strong attraction for the young. For this reason among others, Charles Taylor was reportedly able to recruit without physical force from each town he took as he approached the capital.

'My friends are joining...' is a common refrain among Sri Lankan Tamil children in the northern LTTE-controlled areas. A Jaffna University professor reported how the LTTE takes a few boys from a school, gives them military training and then puts them back in the school. They parade around talking about guns and soon others want to join. This professor's own 13-year-old joined the LTTE dreaming of the glamorous training he had heard about from classmates; he changed his mind, once inside and assigned to kitchen-duty.[48]

2.2.4 Developmental processes

2.2.4.1 Feelings of helplessness

Joining an armed group might attract persons attempting to avoid apparently inevitable dangers, as well as those who feel trapped, powerless, and voiceless but want to influence the factors controlling their lives. Life in a refugee camp often engenders such sentiments. In the late 1970s and early 1980s, when death squad activity was at its height in El Salvador, many

---

47   D. Kuttab, 'A Profile of the Stonethrowers,' above note 32, at 15.
48   Information on Liberia, the occupied territories or Sri Lanka that is not attributed directly to a source, was collected by Ilene Cohn during field investigations and interviews.

youth aged 15-25 joined the FMLN to avoid becoming another disappearance statistic. The 'hopelessness experienced by youth [in Sri Lanka's central district] who see no future for themselves on privatized tea estates, has prompted an increase in the number of young people who consider seriously the LTTE option.'[49] Some Palestinian psychologists and childcare workers insist their children's political consciousness is a product of desperation and dispossession. One Gaza psychiatrist says his patients, young intifada victims, assert they will continue to throw stones at soldiers they encounter because they are convinced that whether they throw stones or not the soldiers will capture and beat them. 'These young people have nothing to lose...If they continue to resist...they will be trying to make a future for themselves...They feel empowered.'[50]

Researchers have traced similar patterns of experience among youth who have grown up to join terrorist groups: Hopelessness that grows into burning rage, a bleak and angry outlook on the future, combined with a critical incident such as arbitrary arrest and torture, witnessing the abuse of persons close to them, or a combination of feelings of guilt and the desire for revenge.[51]

2.2.4.2 Feelings of vulnerability

Feelings of helplessness often go hand-in-hand with feelings of vulnerability. In eastern Sri Lanka some children join the LTTE after seeing their family or a neighbour's family abused, detained, beaten, or killed by the army. The detention and disappearance of Tamil youth has been going on for ten years. According to Asia Watch, 'especially since 1983, Tamil men in the north and east, particularly those between the ages of 15 and 30, were subjected to mass arrests. Hundreds of such people "disappeared" after arrest by security forces...The most serious instances of "disappearances"...are cases where the security forces killed groups of Tamil youths in reprisal for attacks by the militants, disposed of the bodies, and then denied having taken anyone into custody.'[52] Asia Watch has also documented the summary execution of 12 and 14 year-old Tamil boys by security forces in 1987. It is thus easy to imagine that young boys and men feel unprotected, insecure and less at risk inside the LTTE. Some blame the army for having indiscriminately bombed and raided schools in the north,

49 'Report of the Canadian Human Rights Mission to Sri Lanka', Toronto, Jan. 1992, p.11.

50 G. Usher, 'Children of Palestine,' *Race and Class*, vol. 32, no.4, April-June 1991, at 3, quoting Assia Habash, co-director of the Early Childhood Resource Center in Jerusalem.

51 D. Goleman, 'The making of a terrorist could begin in childhood,' *Int'l Herald Tribune*, 12 Sept. 1986.

52 *Cycles of Violence: Human Rights in Sri Lanka since the Indo-Sri Lanka Agreement*, Asia Watch, Washington, D.C. (1987) pp.31-2.

alienating youth and heightening the sense of insecurity. This is especially true in the displaced persons camps where, according to a Red Barna (Norwegian Save the Children) employee with camp experience, youth join the LTTE to avoid the constant army harassment. At the same time, the LTTE's intelligence enables them to warn civilians of impending army offensives, resulting in increased dependence on the separatist LTTE for protection.

2.2.4.3 The desire for revenge

The desire for revenge often originates in personal experiences of physical abuse, torture, killing, disenfranchisement, deprivation, and humiliation. The UNICEF Representative in Uganda in 1985 described NRA child soldiers as 'highly motivated, reliable and dedicated, often instilled with a strong sense of revenge triggered by the UNLA atrocities against their families, friends or village which had driven them to the NRA in the first place.'[53] Many Liberian boys in the NPFL, orphaned during Doe's brutal counter-insurgency campaign, joined voluntarily out of a desire for vengeance.[54] A Liberian human rights worker claimed that some parents volunteered their children to the INPFL (a splinter group of the NPFL) out of a desire to revenge tribal disputes, or in defence of their tribe. An Israeli former prosecutor in Jerusalem during the *intifada* said many 14-15 year-old detainees explained their participation in mass stone throwing as a response to the killing of a fellow villager by the police or military. A Palestinian psychologist with the YMCA's rehabilitation project agreed that many youth want revenge for specific events. A Sri Lankan Tamil from Jaffna, who insisted that children join the LTTE for nationalistic reasons, revealed that in 1988 his own son had run off to the LTTE because a teacher at his school had been shot; he wanted revenge, felt insecure, and in turn had been harassed by anti-LTTE Tamil armed groups trying to recruit him.

The desire for revenge can also be instilled or exacerbated by religious or military leaders, teachers and parents, as the experiences of Iranian and Afghan children confirm.

2.2.4.4 Identity formation

Researchers have predicted that adolescents in certain circumstances forge their sense of identity on the basis of nationalist ideology. Nationalism is indeed an important influence on the emerging identities of children in

---

53 Cole P. Dodge, Magne Raundalen, *Reaching Children in War: Sudan, Uganda and Mozambique*, above note 9, at 53.
54 Interview with IGNU Minister of Defense.

refugee camps, 'where the quest to reclaim their homelands can provide a purpose for living where much else in life conspires to take other purposes away.'[55] For example, James Garbarino sees the intifada as offering a sense of mission or control in life to Palestinians who might otherwise become depressed and without hope in the refugee camps.[56] Another commentator recently noted that every Palestinian determines his or her identity by affiliation with a larger political group.[57]

Some Salvadoran children followed their siblings or relatives to the FMLN, while other combatants are children of guerilla fighters and were literally born into the rebel movement. Some ex-combatants will have spent their entire adolescent and young adult lives in the FMLN, forming valued identities tied to roles as fighters, political or military leaders, or technicians, in an environment that no longer exists. With the coming of peace, they must adjust to the more mundane demands of family or community life, and develop new social and survival skills. Not all will successfully transition through a process they may find depressing, exasperating or overwhelming; similar outcomes have occurred or are foreseeable in other long-running conflicts, such as Nicaragua, Lebanon, Angola, Mozambique, the Philippines, and Cambodia.

55   Neil Boothby and John Humphrey, above note 22.
56   James Garbarino, 'A Note on Children and Youth in Dangerous Environments: The Palestinian Situation as a Case Study.' Erikson Institute, Chicago (undated), p.10.
57   S. Emerson, 'Meltdown: The end of the Intifada', *The New Republic*, p.26 (23 Nov. 1992).

3

Preventing the Recruitment or Participation of Children and Youth in Armed Conflict: Law, Programmes, and Policy

Yann Gamblin – UNICEF
Uganda, 1986. Eleven years old.

Michael Stravato – AP Photo
Rosario, El Salvador, 1991. Young FMLN soldier.

Larry Towell – MAGNUM
Guatemala, 1984. On civilian patrol.

Jim Worrall – TREVETHICK
Northern Iraq, 1991. Young Kurd soldier.

Dexter Cruez – AP Photo
Karadiyawaru, Sri Lanka, 1990. Tamil Tigers.

Donna DeCesare – IMPACT VISUALS
El Salvador, September 1988. Curious children surround young guerillas.

Linda Miller
Morazan, El Salvador, 1989. Young FMLN soldiers on the march.

Eli Reed – MAGNUM
Lebanon, 1983. Young PLO member with rocket launcher.

Yann Gamblin – UNICEF
Uganda, 1986. NRA soldier – 9 years old.

THERE IS NO SINGLE SOURCE for the international law of the child, which means it must be looked for in specific and general treaties, in the broad field of human rights at both universal and regional levels, in the rules of international humanitarian law, in customary international law and in the law and practice of States.

3.1 The International Law of the Child: The Sources of the Law

In 1924, the League of Nations adopted the first declaration on the rights of the child, stressing the need for special care and protection. Though followed by a series of similar and related declarations,[1] another sixty-five years were to pass before the international community acknowledged the very special status of children, and the desirability of States entering into a treaty on their behalf. The 1989 UN Convention on the Rights of the Child, already ratified by some 144 States, is rightly recognized as a critical milestone in the legal protection of children.

At an earlier stage, in 1948, the United Nations adopted the *Universal Declaration of Human Rights*, a non-binding instrument since followed by both regional and global treaties in which States have accepted formal, legal obligations with respect to a wide range of *human rights*. These include the two 1966 Covenants, on Civil and Political Rights and Economic, Social and Cultural Rights; the 1951 Convention and 1967 Protocol relating to the Status of Refugees, and the 1984 Convention against Torture and Other Cruel, Inhuman or Degrading Treatment or Punishment. All provisions in these instruments pertain to children, except for specific articles codifying rights of political participation extended only to those over a certain age. In addition, regional organizations have promoted local systems of obligation and supervision, for example, under the 1950 European Convention on Human Rights, the 1969 American Convention on Human Rights, and the 1981 African Convention on Human and Peoples' Rights. The rules of *international humanitarian law* are found, in particular, in the four 1949 Geneva Conventions and the two 1977 Additional Protocols, as well as in the practices of States and the resolutions of the International Conference of the Red Cross and Red Crescent. Even where a State has not ratified or consented to any particular treaty, it may still be bound by rules that have acquired the status of *customary international law*, for example, because of convergence of the practice of States over time and the accompanying sense

---

1   See for example the 1959 UN Declaration on the Rights of the Child and the 1974 UN Declaration on the Protection of Women and Children in Emergencies and Armed Conflicts.

of legal obligation.[2]

The international law of the child as a whole must be understood *in context*, that is, as a body of rules operating primarily between States, and generally having only an indirect effect on non-State actors such as individuals, 'non-government entities'[3] (NGEs) or other groups; however, this does not exclude the possibility of individual liability for breaches of the law. By contrast, the *international humanitarian law* of internal armed conflicts applies equally to government armed forces and dissident armed groups, that is, to the 'parties to the conflict.'[4] Where there are gaps or contradictions, as often happens when humanitarian need is opposed to military necessity, the long-standing Martens clause, one of the clearest examples of a rule of customary international law in this field, recalls and confirms the most basic standard. In the words of Additional Protocol I:

> In cases not covered by this Protocol or by other international agreements, civilians and combatants remain under the protection and authority of the principles of international law derived from established custom, from the principles of humanity and from the dictates of public conscience.

Children, whether victims or participants in armed conflicts, are thus protected and their liberties ensured, at least in theory, by international and national law. The specific provisions of international law regulating the recruitment and participation of children in armed conflict turn on a number of factors, however, including the type of conflict, ratification of or accession to the relevant treaties. The status of the party recruiting or employing children in its ranks may also be at issue, so far as the applicability of rules other than those of international humanitarian law is concerned.

3.2   International Law and the Child Soldier

3.2.1 Characterizing Conflicts: The Limited Scope of International Humanitarian Law

The 1949 Geneva Conventions anticipate two different types of conflict: First, 'all cases of declared war or any other armed conflict which may arise

---

2   Many of the rules governing the conduct of warfare have their basis in or have become customary international law.

3   This somewhat inelegant phrase is used to include, in particular, political and military movements engaged in power struggles within particular States.

4   See *Common Article 3* of the Four Geneva Conventions.

between two or more High Contracting Parties, even if the state of war is not recognized by one of them',[5] in which the four Conventions apply in their entirety; and secondly, 'the case of armed conflict not of an international character occurring in the territory of one of the High Contracting Parties,' in which the minimum standards of Common Article 3 apply. Examples of the former category include the wars between Iran and Iraq, Cambodia and Vietnam, Panama and the United States, Azerbaijan and Armenia, and the Gulf War. The Fourth Geneva Convention also applies in situations of total or partial occupation, as in the case of the Israeli occupied territories.

The Additional Protocols of 1977 resulted from an initiative of the International Committee of the Red Cross to 'update' the laws of war and, in particular, to encourage States to recognize and accept the changed face of warfare, particularly given the incidence of wars of national liberation and the increasing use of guerilla tactics. The Additional Protocols include provisions limiting the permissible means and methods of combat, strengthening protection of the civilian population, and extending the applicability of international humanitarian law within State boundaries.[6] *Additional Protocol I* expands the concept of international armed conflict,[7] while *Additional Protocol II* applies a limited range of international standards to situations of internal confrontation of a particular level of intensity that is, to what most people would call 'civil war'.

When it was drafted, article 1(4) of *Additional Protocol I* had a largely political content and purpose, being specifically aimed at racist and colonial regimes and alien occupation;[8] its scope today may seem very limited, for

---

5   1949 Geneva Conventions, common article 2. Pursuant to this provision, international humanitarian law also applies 'to all cases of partial or total occupation of the territory of a High Contracting Party, even if the said occupation meets with no armed resistance.' The Fourth Geneva Convention deals in detail with occupation and the treatment of the inhabitants.

6   See, Bedjaoui, M., 'Humanitarian law at a time of failing national and international consensus'; Abi-Saab, G., 'Respect of Humanitarian Norms in International Conflicts;' Cassese, A., 'Respect of Humanitarian Norms in Non-International Conflicts;' in Independent Commission on International Humanitarian Issues, *Modern Wars*, 1986, 1, 60, 86.

7   Art. 1(4), Additional Protocol I, provides that in addition to international armed conflicts described in common article 2 of the Conventions, the category shall include 'armed conflicts in which peoples are fighting against colonial domination and alien occupation and against racist regimes in the exercise of their right to self-determination, as enshrined in the Charter of the United Nations and the Declaration on Principles of International Law concerning Friendly Relations and Co-operation among States in accordance with the Charter of the United Nations.'

8   None of these terms admits of easy application; see Bothe, M., Partsch, K.J. & Solf, W.A., *New Rules for Victims of Armed Conflicts*, 1982, 5-2; Wilson, Heather A., *International Law and the Use of Force by National Liberation Movements*, Oxford, 1988, ch. 7.

few entities engaged in violent liberation or secession struggles[9] have been able to invoke its terms. Even in the few cases where *Additional Protocol I* might apply on the facts, as in the conflict between Western Sahara and Morocco or that between East Timor and Indonesia, neither the States nor the liberation movements have ratified or declared their adherence to the treaty. The actual scope of *Additional Protocol I* will require review, however, if the nationalist and ethnic struggles now emerging from the breakup of established States acquire any degree of international recognition.

An internal conflict will only be subject to the rules laid down in Additional Protocol II, if it reaches a certain level of intensity,[10] and the armed opposition in turn meets the criteria of responsible command, control over territory and capacity to implement the Protocol. Specifically, *Additional Protocol II* extends to conflicts,

> which take place in the territory of a High Contracting Party between its armed forces and dissident armed forces or other organized armed groups which, under responsible command, exercise such control over a part of its territory as to enable them to carry out sustained and concerted military operations and to implement this Protocol.[11]

El Salvador and the Philippines are the only two examples of recent or current conflicts in which both the States and the NGEs have formally accepted the application of *Additional Protocol II*. Although Liberia has ratified the Protocol and the facts warrant its application, the interim government does not have the capacity to implement its provisions and the other parties to the conflict have not accepted its application. In principle, because Liberia is a party to *Additional Protocol II* and the criteria of article 1(1) have been met, with respect to some NGEs at least, its recruitment provisions also apply to non-governmental actors.

Many situations of internal conflicts fall short of the Additional Protocol II threshold, and remain governed by the minimal conditions of

9   Eleven national liberation movements recognized by the League of Arab States and the Organization of African Unity were invited to the Diplomatic Conference convened in 1974 to consider the draft Protocols: African National Congress (ANC), Angola National Liberation Front (FNLA), Mozambique Liberation Front (FRELIMO), People's Movement for the Liberation of Angola (MPLA), Palestine Liberation Organization (PLO), Panafricanist Congress (PAC), Seychelles People's United Party (SPUP), South West Africa People's Organization (SWAPO), Zimbabwe African National Union (ZANU), Zimbabwe African People's Union (ZAPU), African National Council of Zimbabwe (ANCZ). Cited with reference to conference documents in Wilson, above note 7, p. 128, n. 123.

10   Additional Protocol II, art. 1(2).

11   Additional Protocol II, art. 1(1).

Article 3, common to the Four 1949 Geneva Conventions, extends a measure of protection to non-international armed conflicts:

In the case of armed conflict not of an international character occurring in the territory of one of the High Contracting Parties, each Party to the Conflict shall be bound to apply, as a minimum, the following provisions:

(1) Persons taking no active part in the hostilities, including members of armed forces who have laid down their arms and those placed *hors de combat* by sickness, wounds, detention, or any other cause, shall in all circumstances be treated humanely, without any adverse distinction founded on race, colour, religion or faith, sex, birth or wealth, or any other similar criteria.

To this end the following acts are and shall remain prohibited at any time and in any place whatsoever with respect to the above-mentioned persons:

(a) violence to life and person, in particular murder of all kinds, mutilation, cruel treatment and torture;

(b) taking of hostages;

(c) outrages upon personal dignity, in particular humiliating and degrading treatment;

(d) the passing of sentences and the carrying out of executions without previous judgment pronounced by a regularly constituted court, affording all the judicial guarantees which are recognized as indispensable by civilized peoples.

Common Article 3 of the four Geneva Conventions and such human rights provisions as have not been subject to derogation. Common Article 3 also has a threshold, however, presupposing a certain level of internal violence without which it too does not apply, although local law and prevailing human rights obligations certainly do,[12] and the high number of victims has made necessary the application of minimum humanitarian rules.

The applicability of some rules of international humanitarian law thus depends on whether the State has ratified the Geneva Conventions or the Additional Protocols, and whether the conflict in question falls within one of five categories:[13] traditional international armed conflicts; *Additional*

12   Because the Convention on the Rights of the Child has no general derogation provision, children within the jurisdiction of States parties are guaranteed much the same, if not more, protection in time of emergency than is provided by Common Article 3; see Ilene Cohn, 'The Convention on the Rights of the Child: What it Means for Children in War,' 3 *Int'l J. Refugee Law* 100 (1991). On the threshold issue, see further below.

13   See Wilson, Heather A., *International Law and the Use of Force by National Liberation Movements*, Oxford, 1988, at 183.

Protocol I article 1(4) conflicts described above, in which the authority representing a people has made a declaration of intention to apply the Conventions and Protocols;[14] *Additional Protocol II* article 1(1) conflicts, described above, between a State and organized armed groups under responsible command; *Common Article 3* conflicts under the 1949 Conventions;[15] and finally riots, internal disorder and tensions subject to national law and minimum international law standards.

There is no determining body, standard or internationally accepted method for characterizing conflicts, and the processes of definition have not contributed to the wider application of international humanitarian law. Most conflicts today are internal and below the threshold for Additional Protocol II. Recent examples involving child participants include the conflicts in Somalia, Afghanistan, Peru, Guatemala, and Myanmar (Burma). Moreover, relatively few States involved in internal hostilities have been willing to abandon their presumptive claim to a free hand in dealing with local threats, so that the applicability of Additional Protocol II is resisted, even where the objective criteria are satisfied. The conflicts in the Sudan, Lebanon, Angola, Mozambique and Sri Lanka, for example, might well have met the Additional Protocol II threshold, but the States in question are not parties and the NGEs have not purported to make any declaration of acceptance. The scope for *legal* protection in a non-international armed conflict or violent internal strife situation is thus much less than in a traditional inter-State conflict. The gaps in the laws of war mean that especially close attention must be given to the rules of customary international law, and other relevant sources of obligation and standards, such as those dealing with human rights.

For the child soldier and for children generally in situations of internal conflict, the application of international humanitarian standards will depend more often on what the ICRC can achieve informally, through its 'right of

---

14   See Protocol I, art. 96, which provides for a unilateral declaration of undertaking to apply the Conventions and API to be made by 'the authority representing a people engaged against a High Contracting Party in an armed conflict of the type referred to in Article 1, paragraph 4'. For comment see Bothe, M., Partsch, K.J. & Solf, W.A., *New Rules for Victims of Armed Conflicts*, 1982, 36-52, 552-7.

15   In *Nicaragua v. United States*, the International Court of Justice considered that *Common Article 3* codified 'customary international law'; it therefore applies whether or not a State has ratified the Geneva Conventions: ICJ *Reports,* 14, 113-14 (1986). Rules binding on every State as a matter of 'peremptory' customary international law are generally referred to as *jus cogens*. There is still considerable controversy regarding the content of this body of law, as well as the criteria which must be satisfied for such rules to come into existence.

humanitarian initiative,' than on the written terms of treaties.[16] The aims in such circumstances include improving the conditions of detention and treatment, recognizing the 'more general norms of humanity which it is up to each person—whether on the side of the government or its opponents—to respect at all times'.[17]

3.2.2 Recruitment and Participation of Children and Youth in International Armed Conflicts

No rule in the Geneva Conventions or Additional Protocol I provides that a child may never become a combatant, but limits are placed instead on the authorities that control the recruitment process. With respect to international armed conflicts in which the State and/or the armed opposition have declared their adherence to Additional Protocol I, Article 77(2) imposes certain limitations on the freedom to recruit. As María Teresa Dutli has observed, this formulation is less mandatory than that proposed to the Diplomatic Conference by the ICRC, which would have obliged the parties to take 'all necessary measures' to prevent participation. Instead, the text now reflects the wish of governments 'to avoid entering into absolute obligations with regard to the voluntary participation of children in hostilities.'[18] Other commentators have expressed similar views, accepting 'a flexible restriction on the acceptance of voluntary service', to the extent that 'voluntary indirect participation in hostilities by children under fifteen would not involve any breach of Art. 77.'[19] The ICRC's draft article, which would have prohibited even indirect participation in hostilities, such as the transmission of information, transport of arms and provision of supplies,

16 There is a substantial body of practice relating to ICRC activities in such situations. In 1921, the Tenth International Conference of the Red Cross adopted a set of principles relating to involvement in social and revolutionary disturbances, a role which was reiterated in Manila in 1981. Article VII of the 1928 Statutes of the International Red Cross and Red Crescent Movement anticipates a continuing role in 'war, civil war or internal strife', and similar endorsements are found in the 1952 revised statutes (article VI), and in article 5(2)(d) of the Statutes adopted in 1986.

17 See 'ICRC Protection and Assistance Activities in Situations not covered by International Humanitarian Law,' *International Review of the Red Cross*, Jan.-Feb. 1988, 9-37; see Chapter 6 below on proposals to establish a code of conduct applicable to situations of internal strife.

18 Dutli, M.T., 'Captured Child Combatants,' *International Review of the Red Cross*, Sept-Oct 1990, 421-34. The Working Group of the Conference Third Committee noted: 'Le paragraphe 2 est un texte de compromis où l'interdiction absolue de recruter les enfants âgés de moins de 15 ans s'accompagne d'une restriction plus souple, en cas d'acceptation de services volontaires, à savoir prendre "toutes les mesures possibles" pour empêcher ces enfants de participer directement aux hostilités. Le groupe de travail a noté que parfois, et surtout dans les territoires occupés et pendant les guerres de libération nationale, il ne serait pas réaliste d'interdire totalement la participation volontaire des enfants âgés de moins de 15 ans.' *Actes de la Conférence diplomatique sur la réaffirmation et le développement du Droit international humanitaire applicable dans les Conflits Armés*, Geneva (1974-1977), vol. XV, p. 546.

19 Bothe, Partsch, & Solf, *New Rules*, p. 476f.

was rejected by States as unrealistic at the time, having regard to the nature of wars of national liberation.

One NGO reported that 'in a number of developing countries, especially in Africa, children of 14 are already adults... In those countries ... boys of 14 would automatically be combatants.'[20] From a physical and psychological perspective, or from that of the law of the child, this is not only manifestly incorrect, but also misses the point of international humanitarian law, which is protection. The equivocation in article 77 on direct/indirect participation is regrettable. When it was drafted, however, it reflected a level of concern and support for wars of national liberation which needs re-examination today in the light of State practice. The review of national systems (see Annex) shows that the majority of States fix 18 as the age for compulsory military service; and that many States which permit voluntary enlistment at a lower age, nevertheless limit the assignment of such recruits to inactive duty.

> *Article 77(2)(c) of Additional Protocol I* provides:
>
> The Parties to the conflict shall take all feasible measures in order that children who have not attained the age of fifteen years do not take a direct part in hostilities and, in particular, they shall refrain from recruiting them into their armed forces. In recruiting among persons who have attained the age of fifteen years but who have not attained the age of eighteen years, the Parties to the conflict shall endeavour to give priority to those who are oldest.

A careful reading of Article 77(2) can also dispel some of the doubts regarding the wording. An important question in the context of both international and non-international armed conflicts is precisely the meaning of the word 'recruit'. María Teresa Dutli states that the word, 'covers both compulsory and voluntary enrolment, which means that the Parties must also refrain from enroling children under fifteen years of age who volunteer to join the armed forces.'[21] This position is well supported by the ordinary meaning of 'recruit', which is to strengthen, reinforce or replenish, irrespective of source or method. What counts for the purposes of Additional Protocol I is the competence to control entry into the armed forces.

---

20   International Union for Child Welfare, cited in Bothe, Partsch, & Solf, *New Rules*, p. 477, n. 14.

21   Dutli, M.T., 'Captured Child Combatants,' above note 18, at 424.

The parties to the conflict are required to take 'all feasible measures' to ensure that children do not take a direct part in hostilities. That which is 'feasible' is that which is capable of being done and, by definition, whatever is under the jurisdiction and control of a party is *prima facie* capable of being done. It will always be 'feasible', for example, for organized fighting forces to have a policy of non-recruitment of children. It may not always be feasible to ensure implementation at every level, however, particularly where forces are dispersed among a population whose younger members themselves actively seek to participate; the challenge here includes giving the broadest dissemination to humanitarian law principles, seeking out alternatives to enlistment or participation, and clarifying the implications of international obligations for those engaged in hostilities.

The parties to the conflict are obliged, in particular, to 'refrain from recruiting' children under fifteen into their own forces. As phrased, this is a clear example of what is *feasible*, because within the authority or competence of the party. Indeed, article 77 is essentially about the limited freedom of parties to the conflict to recruit or involve children, while recognizing that a child who does participate in hostilities as a member of the armed forces should not lose combatant status and its consequential entitlements.

The treaty obligation for parties, when recruiting from those aged between fifteen and eighteen years, to 'endeavour' to give priority to the oldest, is weaker even than the earlier 'all feasible measures' provision. It may give States, the ICRC and concerned outsiders a legal basis for recommendatory interventions,[22] but will stand for little more unless strengthened from other quarters. It is particularly significant, therefore, that national legislation and the practice of States, especially since 1977, support an increased threshold of protection, in favour of young persons up to the age of 18.[23]

There are no recent conflicts in which Additional Protocol I has been applied to the benefit of child soldiers, generally because one or both of the parties to the conflict has not ratified it or made the necessary declaration. Such was the case in the war between Iran and Iraq, and that between Ethiopia and Eritrea. In the view of the International Committee of the Red Cross and other States parties, the Fourth Geneva Convention applies to the

22   Dutli, above note 18, at 424.
23   Art. 32(1), 1989 Convention on the Rights of the Child, obliges States parties to protect children and young persons from involvement in hazardous work, work that interferes with education, or which is 'harmful to health, or physical, mental, spiritual, moral or social development.' Many States have also subscribed to detailed protection standards governing child labour; see International Labour Organisation, 10 *Conditions of Work Digest*, (1991); also art. 3, ILO Convention No. 138.

Israeli occupied territories, obliging Israel to respect the rights of the Palestinians as 'protected persons'. Neither of the Additional Protocols has been ratified by Israel, however, and it is not clear what legal effect can be attributed to the PLO's 1982 statement of intention to respect the rules of international humanitarian law.[24] Given the criteria explained above, *intifada*-related violence would not amount to 'hostilities' within the meaning of Additional Protocol I; and though they are actively involved in the resistance, children are not being formally recruited.

3.2.3 Recruitment and Participation of Children and Youth in Non-International Armed Conflicts

The *formal* immunity of children from recruitment and 'involvement' is stronger in the civil war situations anticipated in *Additional Protocol II*, even if its application is often obstructed by threshold issues and complex language. Article 4(3)(c) provides that 'children who have not attained the age of fifteen years shall *neither* be recruited in the armed forces or groups *nor* allowed to take part in hostilities'. Two distinct obligations of conduct apply,[25] and voluntary or indirect participation of those under fifteen is equally ruled out.[26] No rule, it is true, *forbids* youth from participating in non-international armed conflicts, which perhaps reflects the practical difficulties of regulating or controlling the self-willed activities of those under eighteen. Instead, responsibility to ensure respect for Additional Protocol II attaches to the parties to the conflict, not to the children; the recruiters, those who have power and/or authority on either the government or opposition side, bear the duty, while any children and young persons who actually do participate in hostilities should continue to receive the protection due to them.

---

24   See Plattner, D., 'La portée juridique des déclarations de respect du droit international humanitaire qui émanent de mouvements en lutte dans un conflit armé,' *Rev. belge dr. int.*, 1984-1985/1, 298-320, at p. 304.

25   'Obligations of conduct' call for action at the level of direct relations between States; the obligation requires a specifically determined course of conduct, and ascertaining whether it has been fulfilled simply turns on whether the State's action or omission is or is not in conformity with the internationally required conduct. 'Obligations of result', on the other hand, implicitly recognize the principle of *choice of means*, especially in the standard-setting context where States are required to bring about a certain situation and enjoy a measure of discretion in determining both what is required and how to achieve the desired result. See Goodwin-Gill, G.S., *The Refugee in International Law*, 1983, 140-48 and sources cited.

26   Bothe, Partsch and Solf attribute the difference in treatment, in part at least, to the fact that 'the provisions for the special protection of children in non-international armed conflict were prepared by Committee I before Committee III undertook the formulation of parallel provisions in Protocol I. In this instance, Committee I followed the ICRC proposal, but Committee III elected to modify it.' *New Rules*, p. 477, n. 16.

From a strictly legal perspective, a non-governmental entity (NGE), like the Government itself, will only be formally bound by Additional Protocol II, if 'its' State has ratified the treaty or, perhaps, if it is recognized as enjoying a sufficient measure of 'personality' and has made a valid unilateral declaration of intent to respect the rules of international humanitarian law.[27] The NGE and its members, as well as government armed forces, will be bound by the rules of customary international law, however, whether they relate to the conduct of hostilities or the general protection of vulnerable groups, such as children. Given the dynamic circumstances of civil war and internal conflict, those rules which are realistically applicable must be carefully identified, and a distinction made between the formal applicability of rules and the consequences of breach. Although no judicial, supervisory or 'enforcement' mechanism may be available, NGE conduct can still be characterised as illegal in appropriate circumstances, with potential consequences for international support and individual responsibility.

The situation in the Philippines shows how difficult it is to invoke Additional Protocol II, because of its complexity, and if neither party formally recognizes its applicability. The Philippines has ratified Additional Protocol II, but the conflict does not fall clearly within its terms, especially given the article 1(1) requirement that the opposition armed forces 'exercise such control over a part of [State] territory as to enable them to carry out sustained and concerted military operations and to implement [the] Protocol.' In its 1990 report, Asia Watch concluded that the opposition New People's Army (NPA) operates under responsible command and is capable of launching operations in all provinces, but doubted the movement's capacity to implement the 'due process' requirements of article 6 of the Protocol.[28] While 'due process' capabilities may indicate an equal capacity to fulfil international obligations, deficiencies in the former

27   See Plattner, above note 24. While NGEs are free to make unilateral declarations, Additional Protocol II contains no formal provision permitting *adherence* in this way.

28   See below, note 34. Common Article 3(1)(d) of the Geneva Conventions prohibits 'the passing of sentences and the carrying out of executions without previous judgment pronounced by a regularly constituted court, affording all the judicial guarantees which are recognized as indispensable by civilized peoples'. Cf. ICRC, *Commentary*, p. 1398, noting that 'some experts argued that it was unlikely that a court could be regularly constituted under national law by an insurgent party.' Compare APII, art. 6(2), which refers to 'a court offering the essential guarantees of independence and impartiality,' and sets out the minimum requirements of due process.

should hardly be used as a reason for not bringing an insurgent group generally within the system of law and protection. Ironically, the interpretation suggested by Asia Watch both denies the applicability of obligations and puts a premium on *disorganization.*[29]

3.2.4 The Participation of Children and Youth in Conflicts beyond the Reach of Humanitarian Law

The theoretical, even idealistic, aspect to much of the discussion of recruitment and employment of children as warriors is dramatically yet consistently highlighted by a comparison of the descriptive information provided in Chapter 2 with the analysis of the law applicable to current conflicts given above. In fact, there are no international armed conflicts today in which children are fighting and to which Additional Protocol I applies. There are far more non-international armed conflicts, but again the problems of compliance remain: Additional Protocol II is often unratified by the State in conflict, *Common Article 3* places no limits on the recruitment or participation of children, the breaches of rules are committed by NGEs, the level of strife is debateable, the applicability of human rights provisions is in doubt, and their enforcement, for various reasons, impossible.

The limited application of existing law to current facts is illustrated by assessments of four recent conflicts. Political repression, insurgency and counter-insurgency have been major features on the landscape of Myanmar since the 1950s, with concerted drives on minority groups seeking greater autonomy dating from 1984. In May 1990, Asia Watch criticized aspects of Myanmar's military practice, including forcible relocations of the population and the 'systematic recruitment of civilians' for portering in support of the army's operations.[30] It would be reasonable to infer that this was a non-international armed conflict to which the rules of international humanitarian law applied. At the time of the report, however, Myanmar had ratified neither the 1949 Geneva Conventions nor the Additional Protocols.[31]

The current conflict in Sri Lanka has all the characteristics of a

29   It is sometimes argued that international obligations bind only States, and not non-State entities, such as unrecognized belligerents or liberation movements. Common Article 3 goes beyond such formalistic arguments, precisely by being addressed to 'parties to the conflict', while APII, art. 1 'develops and supplements' this provision with respect to armed conflicts between a government's armed forces and 'dissident armed forces or other organized armed groups...' Note also the long-accepted dimension of *individual* responsibility for violations of international humanitarian law; see sections 5.1.3. and 5.1.4 below.

30   *Human Rights in Burma (Myanmar)*, Asia Watch, NY, May 1990.

31   Myanmar subsequently ratified the Geneva Conventions on 25 Aug. 1992.

non-international armed conflict; on the facts, Additional Protocol II would seem to apply, save that Sri Lanka is not a party. Children and youth are being recruited only by the secessionist Tamil forces, the LTTE, which, in the absence of ratification or effective unilateral declaration, is not bound by its provisions.

Asia Watch's approach in both cases has been to 'apply' the rules notwithstanding, on the assumption, first, that *Common Article 3* was a rule of such a fundamental character in international law as to be binding irrespective of formal consent, such as ratification of treaty;[32] and secondly, that Additional Protocol II anyway provides 'authoritative guidance' on the conduct of hostilities. 'Guidance', however, is a far cry from obligation, and yields rather too easily to counter-arguments based on military necessity, particularly where none of the parties to the conflict has expressed any interest in applying rules.

The situations in El Salvador and the Philippines therefore provide useful comparisons, but equally troubling outcomes as concerns child soldiers. While the facts in El Salvador came much closer to meeting the Additional Protocol II threshold than those in the Philippines, in both cases the government and the insurgents[33] stated their willingness to be bound by its provisions.[34] Nevertheless, for many years the El Salvadoran armed forces recruited youth under eighteen, and Filipino youth continue to participate in paramilitary forces. In both countries children and youth were also either recruited or voluntarily enlisted in opposition groups.

3.2.5 The Convention on the Rights of the Child and the Child Soldier

As a document, the Convention on the Rights of the Child (CRC) certainly offers substantial *general* support for the argument against recruitment. Indeed, article 29 on the aims of education offers a platform almost incompatible by definition with the involvement of children in armed

---

32 See footnote 16 above, and text.

33 In El Salvador, the FMLN and in the Philippines, the New People's Army (NPA).

34 *The Philippines. Violations of the Laws of War by both Sides,* Asia Watch, August 1990, pp. 10, 15. On 15 Aug. 1991, the NPA sent a statement informing the ICRC of the NPA 'desire to comply with international humanitarian law, in particular article three common to the Geneva Conventions and Additional Protocol II.' International Committee of the Red Cross, *Annual Report 1991.*

conflict.[35] In this respect, it complements the provisions of international humanitarian law with respect to education, and contemplates the broad dissemination of such law and principles as a preventive measure.

Article 12 of the Convention obliges States Parties to 'assure to the child who is capable of forming his or her own views the right to express those views freely in all matters affecting the child, the views of the child being given due weight in accordance with the age and maturity of the child.' None of the national legal systems reviewed satisfies this requirement, either with respect to compulsory service or the assignment of volunteer soldiers to active duty.

Article 38 of the Convention, refers to applicable humanitarian law and limits the recruitment and participation of children in armed conflicts in

---

Article 38, Convention on the Rights of the Child

(1) States Parties undertake to respect and to ensure respect for rules of international humanitarian law applicable to them in armed conflicts which are relevant to the child.

(2) States Parties shall take all feasible measures to ensure that persons who have not attained the age of fifteen years to not take a direct part in hostilities.

(3) States Parties shall refrain from recruiting any person who has not attained the age of fifteen years into their armed forces. In recruiting among those persons who have attained the age of fifteen years but who have not attained the age of eighteen years, States Parties shall endeavour to give priority to those who are oldest.

(4) In accordance with their obligations under international humanitarian law to protect the civilian population in armed conflicts, States Parties shall take all feasible measures to ensure protection and care of children who are affected by an armed conflict.

---

familiar language. The 25th International Conference of the Red Cross, held in Geneva in 1986, stressed that the protection to be provided by the convention on the rights of the child, then under consideration, 'should be

---

35   Among other aims, States parties agree in art. 29 that the education of the child should be directed to '(b) The development of respect for human rights and fundamental freedoms, and for the principles enshrined in the Charter of the United Nations; (c) The development of respect for the child's parents, his or her own cultural identity, language and values ... and for civilizations different from his or her own; (d) The preparation of the child for responsible life in a free society, in the spirit of understanding, peace, tolerance, equality of sexes, and friendship among all peoples, ethnic, national and religious groups and persons of indigenous origin.'

at least the same as that accorded by the Geneva Conventions and the two Additional Protocols.'[36] It did not work out quite that way, with the United States representative taking the position that a provision of international humanitarian law should not be altered by a human rights instrument.[37] So, while incorporating most of article 77(2) of Additional Protocol I, article 38 of the CRC qualifies article 4(3) of Additional Protocol II, by requiring that States Parties take all feasible measures to prevent only the child's *direct participation in hostilities.*

Where both the CRC and the Additional Protocols have been ratified, CRC article 41 ensures that the discrepancies in the wording noted above will not diminish the protection afforded children.[38] Children's rights monitors will need to check a State's compliance with the CRC against the highest protective standard, whether it is found in national or relevant international law.

Like most human rights treaties, the CRC is limited in that it is directed to States, rather than to the parties to a conflict. When a conflict is beyond the reach of international humanitarian law for any reason, the CRC may yet be the way to bring those standards in through the back door. For example, Guatemala has national legislation setting eighteen as the minimum age for conscription, but still children are recruited into the armed forces and the civil patrols. Guatemala is nevertheless a party to the CRC, which offers a specific channel to challenge its policy and practice. In many other similar situations where children participate in armed opposition groups and *Additional Protocol II* does not apply, the fact that the State has ratified the Convention on the Rights of the Child, as is the case in Sri Lanka, Peru, the Sudan, and Myanmar (Burma), presents the double challenge of extending the law to the NGEs and monitoring their compliance.

Whether the vast potential of the UN Convention on the Rights of the Child is ever realised will depend both on the seriousness with which States approach implementation and on the success of the Committee on the Rights

---

36   See Resolution No. IX, Point 7, cited in Françoise Krill, 'The Protection of Children in Armed Conflict,' in Freeman, M. and Veerman, P., *The Ideologies of Children's Rights*, (1992), 347-56. See also the views submitted to the Working Group on the draft convention by Rädda Barnen International: UN doc. E/CN.4/1987/WG1/WP.3; and by ICRC: UN doc. E/CN.4/1987/WG1/WP.4.

37   In debates on article 38 of the Convention on the Rights of the Child, the U.S. delegate refused to accept substituting either 'necessary' or 'possible' for the word 'feasible', but gave few reasons for this position. He asserted that to adopt the higher standard might even oblige an invaded State to renounce self-defence: UN doc. E/CN.4/1989/WG.1/L.54, para. 592. Not surprisingly, such extreme arguments beg the question of surrender. Ironically, the United States itself requires parental consent for volunteers under eighteen, and does not assign those under eighteen to combat duty.

38   Article 41 provides that 'Nothing in the present Convention shall affect any provisions which are more conducive to the realization of the rights of the child and which may be contained in: (a) The law of State Party; or (b) International law in force for that State.'

of the Child as a monitoring mechanism. Already, however, the Committee has identified the child soldier and the child in war as subjects calling for urgent attention,[39] and its strong future support for the campaign against child participation can be expected.

3.2.6 Summary of Legal Arguments against the Recruitment and Participation of Children and Youth

Only children who do not take part in hostilities are entitled to benefit from the regime of special protection established by the Geneva Conventions and Additional Protocols. If they do participate, they lose their inviolability as non-combatants; indeed, they become 'legitimate' military targets, individuals whose death or disablement results in that weakening of the armed forces of the enemy which is the only legitimate aim in war.[40] To conscript or recruit soldiers, of whatever age, is necessarily to change their status; to convert them from civilians, in Michael Walzer's words, 'immune to start with ... [whose] right not to be attacked is a feature of normal human relationships,' to fighters who can be personally attacked on that account alone.[41]

There is a sufficient body of international customary law, drawing from humanitarian law, the law of human rights and the law of the child, that now applies to international and internal conflicts, no matter the level of violence. In a paper published in September 1989, Rädda Barnen threw light on the article 38 debate by showing how the non-substantive objections of the United States of America and the USSR prevailed over the more protective approach of some twenty-four other States and the ICRC on the issue of age, and some eighteen other States and the ICRC on the measures to be taken to protect children affected.[42] The present text, which reflects a minimal 'consensus', is nonetheless important for the consolidation that it brings to the rule of customary international law.[43] Knowingly to allow or to require the participation in conflict of children under fifteen years of age is a violation of their human rights under customary international law, no

---

39   See below, section 6.2.3.

40   Cf. Declaration of St. Petersburg, 1868.

41   Walzer, M., *Just and Unjust Wars*, 1977, 145f, note.

42   See Rädda Barnen, 'No Child Soldiers!' Sept. 1989. This paper, which includes a detailed memorandum by Defence for Children—International, was a last-ditch effort to persuade governments to amend article 38 of the draft convention.

43   A U.S. Joint Chiefs of Staff expert, speaking in a personal capacity at a panel in 1989, identified API art. 77 as among the 'likely candidates eventually to reflect general practice recognized as law.' Quoted with references in Meron, T., *Human Rights and Humanitarian Norms as Customary Law*, 1989, pp. 64-6. The terms of CRC art. 38 are almost identical to those of API art. 77.

matter that the child 'volunteers'. Young persons between fifteen and eighteen years also benefit in principle from the rule requiring non-enrolment and non-participation. The exceptions recognized in the 1977 Additional Protocols and the 1989 Convention on the Rights of the Child must be interpreted in the light of State practice, specifically legislation, which generally accepts eighteen as the minimum age, and the guiding principle of the best interests of the child. The possibilities for clarification and improvement in the rules and in methods for monitoring and implementation are examined in Chapter 6 below.

The general tendency to adopt legislation against conscription below the age of eighteen, considered together with an emerging practice of not assigning volunteers under eighteen to active service, gives a clearer picture of where the law now stands. Strengthened by the rules and general policy of the CRC and other universal and regional human rights instruments, the principle of protecting children and young persons from involvement in armed conflict supplements the traditional scope of international humanitarian law.

Reviewing the sources and content of international humanitarian law and the law of the child nevertheless helps us to restate the entitlement of the child to be immune from recruitment or enrolment. In principle, rules that seem to exist at some remote inter-State level, in fact also have their impact on groups and individuals in their mutual relations. The extent to which dissident armed opposition groups, for example, may be 'bound' by international humanitarian law is a functional issue, not a question of standing or legitimacy.

The practical question for legislators, policy-makers and military commanders is the extent to which the 'military necessity' reflected in personnel requirements ought ever to prevail over the survival of a generation. Military necessity cannot provide a justification for conscription or the use of children in combat. That issue is likely to be resolved, not by the formal provisions of international humanitarian law, but in the practice of States and at least some non-government entities. The challenge for advocates for the child is to influence that practice, by ensuring that standards of protection, no matter what their source, are sufficiently incorporated.

The major problems remain: first, that of opposing the principle to the practice of States and, in particular, the practice of guerilla organizations and other non-recognized entities; and second, the elimination of the factors that motivate children to seek entry into armed groups, as discussed above in Chapter 2. Many current conflicts oppose precisely the reality of children under arms to the ideal of applied rules, and expose the limits of a normative approach in situations where institutional capacity for rehabilitation, accommodation or alternatives is deficient or simply lacking.

3.3   Preventing the Recruitment or Participation of Children and Youth

Prevention strategies need to reflect the many and complex ways in which children and adolescents come to participate in hostilities: they must address the macro issues of the conflict, as well as the more subjective factors personal to the child and his or her ecology. These are long-term, multifaceted undertakings, with implications far broader in scope than merely inhibiting recruitment.

The following pages propose arguments, strategies, policies and programmes, aimed at reducing the participation of children in armed conflict. We also examine several concrete efforts made by different types of actors, including international agencies and local non-governmental organizations (NGOs). Interventions may be effective over the short or long-term, they may target forced recruitment or volunteerism, and they can be implemented by a range of different actors.

Motivations for forced recruitment include: population control, ethnic, class or racial discrimination. The recruits are commonly identified as young, impressionable, poor, un- or under-educated, indigenous, and/or rural. Many factors that generate conflict, such as discrimination and social injustice, are reflected in the forced recruitment practices of some governments. Manpower shortages are also relevant factors for both governments and non-State entities. Whether the need to fill the ranks will be satisfied through forced recruitment of youth depends on various elements, including a balancing of the ultimate goals against the risks to young fighters, the level of concern for troop morale and the subsequent level of desertions. It would be difficult to build a strategy for reducing recruitment by trying to convince commanders of the strategic importance of high troop morale or by encouraging desertions. Depending on the fervour with which a conflict is fought and the objectives of the adults, it can be difficult to counteract recruitment as a consequence of manpower shortages. The Center on War and the Child cited manpower needs as outweighing the impact of all the negative publicity Iran received in the international press for its abusive employment of youth in the war with Iraq.[44] Which may also explain why 'even handicapped children have been recruited to explode land mines in front of advancing tanks and adult troops.'[45]

Examples of strategies that attempt to break the pattern of forced recruitment by government forces include legal action on behalf of youth illegally or arbitrarily conscripted. Interventions intended to minimize voluntary participation, include those which indirectly address volunteerism by targeting structural problems, and those more directly attempting to change perceptions of the value of participation held by youth and members of their ecologies. Among the former are the use of international donor pressure, informing international public opinion on the relationship between the participation of children and the root causes of the conflict, or international legal proceedings. Examples of the latter include strengthening those members of a child's ecology who can influence a child's perception of the value of participation, or identifying alternative outlets for the emotions that drive a young person to volunteer.

3.3.1 Intervention to Eliminate Forced Recruitment by Government Forces: Developments in Central America

Forced participation in civil patrols, such as those in Guatemala and Peru, and forced recruitment into any armed force or group, violates human dignity and integrity and the rights to freedom of association and freedom of movement. Recruitment is generally not subject to legal challenge or judicial review, and conscientious objection is rarely an option.

NGOs in Guatemala are increasingly united and active in the battle against forced recruitment by the army and the PACs. Recruitment of minors into either group is both illegal and procedurally discriminatory.[46] Peasant Unity Committee (CUC) leaders insist that young men 'know the dangers of being recruited into the army', and report that more and more youth simply refuse to go. Consequently they risk being rounded up, detained, and forced into the barracks. The Archbishop's Human Rights Office, among others, has challenged these practices in the Inter-American Commission on Human Rights, arguing that detained draft evaders should be charged and receive due process, not forced service. Although families cannot afford the 'price' of their sons' release and language and finances prohibit many families from searching for a recruited son, the women in some villages have reportedly surrounded recruiting soldiers, actually obliging them to

---

44   *Christian Science Monitor*, 28 Oct. 1987.

45   Neil Boothby, 'The New Face of War,' unpublished paper adapted from *War and Refugee Children*, Oxford University Press, p.7

46   Guatemalan national law provides for conscription at age 18; the recruitment process takes the form of arbitrary detention, primarily of young indigenous peasants and the poor.

leave.[47]

In the department of Sololá, Guatemala, an indigenous human rights NGO was formed in 1992 to address violations of cultural rights, the rights to life and physical liberty. Their first initiative, a challenge to forced recruitment, began with open meetings in each village and the collection of some 9,845 signatures on a petition alleging that obligatory service violates cultural rights, proposing alternative social service options, insisting on cessation of intimidation and reprisals against indigenous persons reluctant to submit to the draft, and indicating that the local army unit would be considered responsible for any harm that might come to the youth who refuse the draft or persons signing the petition.

According to the NGO's leaders, the local military commander responded by declaring the petition unconstitutional, giving the petitioners a tour of soldiers' accommodation, and attempting to persuade them that parents need not worry about their recruited sons' living conditions. After unsuccessful visits to the governor and the mayor, the group petitioned Congress, the Ministry of Defence, the President and the Human Rights Ombudsman. As the communities began to prepare for an armed confrontation with army recruiters, a representative of the Human Rights Ombudsman's office negotiated a settlement guaranteeing no further recruitment in Sololá Department in 1993. The group's unexpected success, at least for the time being, shows the importance of grass roots organization around issues of immediate concern. Issue-specific interventions or pressures may impede recruitment of youth and then serve as a springboard for addressing larger macro issues, such as discrimination, racism, or militarism in society.

Besides community organization and popular, mass protests, the legal routes are also being tested in Guatemala. In cases of under-age recruitment where minors often have no documentation of their age, advocates must first make a successful demand for habeas corpus (for the personal appearance of the recruit), and then argue that the legal presumption in favour of the youth's under-age status be respected. NGOs have moved from a position on the non-discriminatory recruitment of adults, to the present demand for an end to mandatory military service, with community service, under civilian direction, as an alternative.[48] They have mounted a campaign for legal reform and in the meantime they are promoting popular resistance to new army recruitment methods.

The Human Rights Ombudsman reported sixty-eight cases of illegal

47   Information collected in interviews conducted in Guatemala by Ilene Cohn.
48   'No al reclutamiento militar forzoso de los jovenes', brochure produced by the Coordinadora Nacional de Viudas de Guatemala (CONAVIGUA), Guatemala.

recruitment of minors in 1992 and 31% of denunciations received by the office of the Children's Rights Ombudsman since December 1990 dealt with the forced recruitment of minors. The Ombudsman's office has charged military authorities with violating the minors' rights to liberty, equality, security, integrity and dignity.[49] Such initiatives on the part of government agencies merit international recognition and technical support.

With respect to the PACs, the popular movement has initiated a drive, using pamphlets,[50] community-based education, marches, and petitions to government officials to promote awareness of why the PACs exist and the many ways in which they violate the rights of those forced to participate without pay. In response, according to one NGO leader, the fields of resisting communities have been burned, ostensibly for drug-control purposes, while soldiers dressed as civilians commit thefts so as to enable the army to argue that the PACs fulfil a necessary police function. The Human Rights Ombudsman publicly denounces recruitment into the PACs as a violation of the freedom of association and blames military commissioners for perpetrating kidnapping, illegal detention, physical injury, threats, property damage and assassinations against resisters.[51]

Legal action against the PAC system has been initiated locally and in the Inter-American Commission for Human Rights. The CERJ (Council of Ethnic Communities), an NGO established in Quiche in 1988, has been translating into Mayan languages and distributing article 34 of the Guatemalan Constitution, which provides for freedom of association and specifies that no one can be obliged to participate in the civil defence patrols. Groups of indigenous highland Guatemalans are now refusing to take part, and a number of resisters have been intimidated, disappeared or assassinated.[52] The CERJ holds human rights seminars in popular language for community representatives from some 120 villages, informing and encouraging people to take action in defence of their civil and political rights. In addition to organizing marches and demonstrations, the CERJ provides legal assistance to families or individuals to obtain the release from military service or PAC duty of a minor or other legally exempted person.

A negotiated solution in the context of the peace talks seems unlikely,

49 *Procurador de Derechos Humanos: Informe Circunstanciado de Actividades y de la Situación de los Derechos Humanos durante 1992*, Guatemala, at 32-33.

50 'Qué son las PAC?' pamphlet produced by the Comite de Unidad Campesina (CUC), Guatemala; 'Documento de Propuestas' pamphlet produced by the Consejo Nacional de Desplazados de Guatemala (CONDEG), January 1993, Guatemala.

51 *Los Derechos Humanos: Un Compromiso por la Justicia y la Paz*, report of the Procurador de los Derechos Humanos, 1987-1992, Guatemala, at 33.

52 See *Persecution by Proxy: The Civil Patrols in Guatemala*, The Robert F. Kennedy Memorial Center for Human Rights, New York, 1993.

as the popular movement is not represented as such. Moreover, the popular movement itself does not believe that government institutions or procedures, such as the Human Rights Ombudsman's office or voting, are able to provide positive results on the recruitment issue.

In El Salvador until recently it was virtually impossible for poor peasant families to challenge successfully the arbitrary recruitment of under-age boys. The United Nations Observer Mission for El Salvador (ONUSAL), established in 1991 and charged in part with monitoring the implementation of a human rights protocol, dealt with the problem of forced recruitment by both parties to the conflict. Any person could complain to ONUSAL at any time, and the allegation was investigated. If it was verified, ONUSAL legal and human rights staff provided the complainant with a form letter citing the relevant legislation or military directive and pleading their case to the appropriate army officer. This procedure was often successful and because it was not done in the name of ONUSAL, local NGOs were able to duplicate and expand the initiative, producing letters addressed to army officers in the name of the injured party.[53] Since July 1992, a new recruitment law provides for mandatory conscription at 18 and voluntary enlistment at 16.

3.3.2 Interventions to Eliminate Coerced or Forced Recruitment by Armed Groups

Unrecognized armed opposition groups have no 'right' to institute a draft, but are nonetheless subject to both national and international law. In practice, major practical problems make it difficult to ensure compliance with the relevant standards. In some cases, negative media publicity can pressure armed groups to conform to international norms. Sometimes armed groups will adhere to even higher standards, in the hope of gaining positive publicity and legitimacy. With respect to Iran, publicity had no effect at all, whereas in El Salvador the opposite was more often true. Sometimes an armed group will recognize that using children is not militarily or strategically beneficial, while at other times, as in Mozambique, the opposite applied. Concerned local NGOs, religious groups or community leaders with access to opposition leaders will therefore need to formulate an appeal based on a moral agenda that reflects local values, custom and practice. International donors, in turn, can consider strengthening such local initiatives, which stand the chance of being most effective when the armed group relies heavily on the local civilian population for support and protection.

---

53   Local NGOs and church groups had for years taken action on behalf of persons arbitrarily and forcibly recruited by the armed forces, but with very limited success.

Perhaps foreign aid donors supporting armed groups have the highest likelihood of pressuring their clients not to recruit youth under eighteen. A Sri Lankan civil rights activist suggested that pressure and a campaign of exposure of the LTTE's use of children could be persuasive, if carried out by the countries in which the LTTE has large expatriate support groups, such as Norway, France, the United Kingdom, Australia, Canada and India. No local groups have taken up the issue and it carries the danger of being exploited by Sinhalese against Tamils. In addition, by pushing the issue of child soldiers, Sri Lankan branches of international NGOs risk losing access to the affected civilian populations in the north and east. The issue might be more effectively dealt with at the headquarters level of international NGOs.

3.3.3 Institutional Interventions: UNHCR and Child Refugees

In 1987, UNHCR put the problems of refugee children on the agenda of its Executive Committee, including the incidence of forcible recruitment, 'from refugee camps to join armed opposition groups in the country of origin or national armed forces of the country of asylum.'[54] UNHCR identified this practice as linked to military or armed attacks on refugee camps and settlements, in violation of their civilian character. In conclusions adopted the same year, the Executive Committee condemned forced recruitment and the exposure of refugee children to physical violence and other violations of their basic rights; it called for appropriate national and international action, including special needs programmes and education.[55] In August 1988, UNHCR issued *Guidelines on Refugee Children,* in which the Office confirmed its policy to intervene with governments to ensure that they defend the safety and liberty of refugee children, but also 'to assume direct responsibility in many situations for protecting the safety and liberty of refugee children.'[56] UNHCR field offices were instructed to promote conditions, such as the location of camps at a reasonable distance from the frontier of their country of origin, so as to ensure the safety of refugee children from attack and forced recruitment;[57] and to report all incidents of recruitment by State armies or guerilla or

54   UNHCR, *Note on Refugee Children*: UN doc. E/SCP/46, 9 Jul. 1987. UNHCR also stated its intention to include within its protection and assistance activities, 'refugees, asylum seekers and displaced persons of concern to UNHCR, up to the age of 18, unless under applicable national law, the age of majority is less.' (Para. 8).

55   Executive Committee Conclusion No. 46; Report of the 38th Session: UN doc. A/AC.96/702, 22 Oct. 1987, para. 205. See also para. 206.4(c), on location of refugee camps and settlements at a reasonable distance from the frontier.

56   UNHCR, *Guidelines on Refugee Children*, Geneva, Aug. 1988, para. 25. The *Guidelines* were being updated during 1993.

57   Ibid., para. 26(b).

insurgent forces, both to the authorities in the country of asylum and to UNHCR Headquarters. 'Recruitment' was defined to include 'not only forced recruitment but also voluntary participation in armed attacks. Equally, support functions, such as carrying arms and ammunition and acting as scouts for military patrols is as unacceptable as more direct functions, such as active combat duty.'[58]

Anders Johnsson, formerly UNHCR Senior Legal Officer, speaking at a media seminar on the Convention on the Rights of the Child in New York in November 1989, referred to a marked increase in instances of recruitment in Africa, Asia and Latin America, involving many thousands of refugee children:[59]

> The recruitment of refugee children into belligerent forces constitutes an unacceptable practice from all perspectives. It places the life and integrity of the child at risk and is contrary to the accepted notions that children must not take a direct part in hostilities and that refugees are civilians and their camps and settlements have a strictly humanitarian and civilian character. UNHCR has intervened in a large number of situations with a view to preventing the forced recruitment of refugee children. Too often, however, national authorities have been unable, or unwilling, to extend the required protection.

The assumption of responsibilities by UNHCR with respect to refugee children at risk of forced recruitment has been confirmed in subsequent conclusions of the Executive Committee.[60] Bearing in mind the scope of UNHCR's mandate, which generally requires an element of international displacement, this positive interventionist role nevertheless has considerable potential.

3.4   Intervention to Reduce Volunteerism

3.4.1 Structural Reform

'We appeal to the government to stop its total war approach and finally to

58   Ibid., para. 26(e).
59   'Refugee Children Today,' Statement by Anders B. Johnsson, Senior Legal Adviser, UNHCR, at the Media Seminar on the Convention on the Rights of the Child organized by the United Nations Centre for Human Rights and the United Nations Children's Fund (UNICEF), New York, 16 Nov. 1989.
60   See the 1989 Conclusion on Refugee Children, in which the Executive Committee called on UNHCR to promote the best possible legal protection for unaccompanied minors, particularly with regard to forced recruitment.

address the roots of the "insurgency" problem, and consequently that of child combatants.'[61] This appeal by Filipino child care specialists to the Filipino government rightly stresses the priority to be given to the structural injustices and violence that generate armed conflict and strife. Throughout the field research for this study, dealing with the root causes has been the only method consistently suggested for reducing youth volunteerism, even though no particular programme or policy has ever appeared to link the two concerns explicitly. Local people and organizations may be at risk if they address such issues, but international donor governments, financial lending institutions, and international aid agencies are better placed to promote structural reform by conditioning aid on government respect for fundamental human rights.

Though in principle participation in an armed group is against the best interests of children, and though children themselves are in no position to determine their best interests before a certain age, successful recommendations for national and international action must improve the circumstances of those youth for whom enrolment is the best available or only perceivable option.

3.4.2 Targeting Children's and their Ecologies' Appraisal of the Decision to Participate

Interventions aimed at how children appraise the decision to participate in a conflict and, in particular, at influencing those around them, must often face the difficulty not just of convincing adults of the many negative consequences attaching to children's involvement in conflict, but of overcoming the conviction that children's participation is inevitable or that the dangers are outweighed by the urgency of the root causes of the conflict.

Filipino psychologists have stressed the importance of materially and emotionally bolstering the extended family and community, which serves as a support system for adults, who in turn mitigate or aggravate a child's ability to cope with stressful events. How adults respond to children's questions about macro social, economic or justice issues, often determines how the child will cope or respond.[62] The question is, how to readjust the value that some adults place on youth participation in hostilities as a response to such issues?[63]

The information on the negative consequences of youth participation

---

61   Elizabeth Marcelino, 'Children at War', *Children of the Storm*, Children's Rehabilitation Center, Manila, July 1991-March 1992, at 3.
62   Ibid.
63   In wars generated purely by ethnic or group hatreds, as in Bosnia & Herzegovina, attention might be paid to ways of readjusting adults' and children's perceptions of the root causes.

provided in Chapter 4 may convince more adults to prevent their children from volunteering as combatants. However, adults may still perceive the goals of conflict as outweighing the risks to children, military leaders may still prefer child soldiers precisely for some of the very reasons we argue against their participation, while others may argue that children are highly resilient and survive better as combatants than as victims. These are some of the challenges for an innovative approach to reducing the numbers of child soldiers.

Can law be used to influence how people regard the use of child soldiers, that is, can the illegality of youth participation influence military leaders? Perhaps an argument can be made, based on *Common Article 3* to the Geneva Conventions, that a young person's physical integrity is violated or unduly at risk by allowing him or her to participate in hostilities. A declaration of minimum standards applicable to all parties in internal armed conflicts and civil strife, as was adopted in Turku/Åbo in 1990, could include a prohibition on the participation of youth under eighteen; it would also enable international donors to make compliance a condition of aid.[64]

Short of relying on legal arguments, perhaps value advocacy based on a moral agenda that includes aspects of local culture, religion or history could be developed. An argument that those with control of territory have a responsibility to the population, and that regardless of their own agenda they should protect children and refuse their participation might be made. Again, this approach is difficult once conflict has broken out. Unfortunately, at that point often only practical limitations on military strategies are respected. Evidence of a military or strategic detriment inherent in having very young soldiers would be useful.

Arguments should be developed to combat the myth of the 'warring culture', emphasizing that children go into war once the normal cultural context has been completely altered and the need to restore pre-war values to the extent that these coincide with international human rights.

Strategies might also be designed to counteract how child soldiers are used for propaganda value. Filipino child care workers, for example, have denounced the fact that both sides in the conflict use the death of child soldiers to mobilize outrage against the enemy and that both sides point to youth volunteerism to encourage adult participation.

3.4.3 Bolstering Children's Feelings of Empowerment and Security
Can alternative means be sought to empower youth and instill feelings of

---

64   In principle, any such move should apply equally to *international armed conflicts*, where the 15-year age limit continues; see further below, pp.149-50.

competence, security and strength? Feelings of helplessness and vulnerability are often not perception problems but very real facts, in which case it is not a matter of making the child *feel* empowered or secure but rather of actually reducing repression and improving his or her security or capacity to effect change without a gun. This may involve interventions as wide-ranging as international denunciation or pressure on governments that commit or sanction disappearances, torture, and intimidation; legal assistance to pursue claims for rights violations; and improved, even internationally monitored security in conflict zones, refugee and displaced persons camps.

Part of the response to the problem will include alternative activities for children in war-zones. If schools could be kept open or recreational activities provided, for example, young people might feel less bored, frustrated, or desperate. It can never be known how many children would not have joined armed groups had their schools been maintained, or their source of income and support continued. However, very few attempts have been made to draw children away from armed groups by offering educational opportunities. Where education is highly valued and parents can afford to continue to send their children to school, it can be assumed that the attractions of joining an armed group are less. But this is not always enough, for in Liberia we found that keeping children in school in the conflict zone merely helped to facilitate recruitment by armed opposition groups.

3.4.4 Encouraging the Demobilization of Child Soldiers

Even where youth regret their decision to volunteer, they often find it impossible to leave an armed group safely. Not only is it hard to leave the Sri Lankan LTTE, but it is also nearly impossible for any civilian to leave the northern zone. Even if deserters can make it to the south, they risk being identified and detained by the police, while their family is subject to harassment and threats in the north. A combatant who merely expresses the desire to leave risks being beaten in front of the other troops. The punishment for requesting permission to quit, for example, involves being sent to dig bunkers in areas under heavy shelling, or three to four months of hard labour breaking stones in Jaffna Fort. Obviously, this may have a general deterrent effect on anyone who thinks of asking to go.

Structural or macro issues are of central importance at the demobilization stage. Land reform, for example, a major cause of the war in El Salvador, remains an issue as ex-combatants grapple with their possibilities for reintegration into civil society. Although agriculture as a means of survival requires no new skills for ex-combatants, and most have chosen the land option within the demobilization package, the quality and quantity of the land offered in such a small, densely populated country, is a matter for debate.

Improved socio-economic conditions will often be a factor in persuading some young soldiers to demobilize. Armed groups in Liberia are not likely to demobilize soon in spite of amnesty offers. The conflict continues, and there is little to induce the vast majority to disarm—no jobs, no infrastructure, and no food. Fear of retribution and uncertainty about the future are also reasons for not disarming. Many soldiers are from rural Liberia and should they disarm now they would be stranded in the capital without family or community support. Family tracing programmes, provision of care for the homeless or orphaned, physical and psychosocial rehabilitation might facilitate demobilization. Assistance directed to families or communities would also ease the burdens of reintegrating ex-combatants.

As one step towards consolidating peace, programmes during the transition phase need to address the training and education of child combatants and adults who have passed their childhood years as combatants, as well as ways in which to link demobilization to local development initiatives.

4

Conditions & Consequences
of Participation

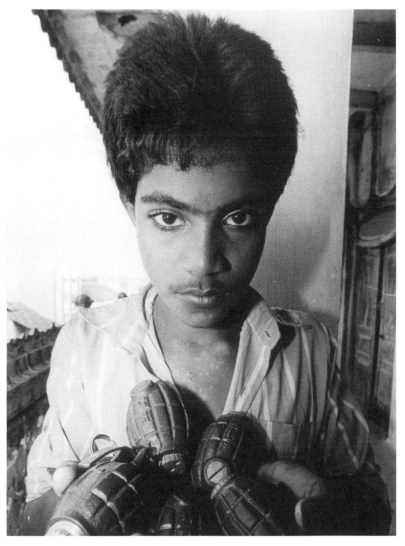

Liu Heung Shing – AP Photo
Jaffna, Sri Lanka, 1987. 16-year old Tamil with locally made grenades.

AP Photo
Jerusalem, 1989. Palestinian boy detained.

Patrick Robert – SYGMA
Liberia, 1992. Rebels with Charles Taylor.

Yann Gamblin – UNICEF
Uganda, 1986. War's aftermath.

Steve McCurry – MAGNUM
Afghanistan, 1986. 12-year old casualty of mines.

Donna DeCesare – IMPACT VISUALS
Los Ranchos, Chalate, El Salvador, May 1992. FMLN training camp.

Susan Meiselas – MAGNUM
Contra Camp, Yamales, Honduras, 1988. Training.

Teit Hornbak – IMPACT VISUALS
Somalia, September 1992. Young clan fighter.

WE INVESTIGATED THE TRAINING PROVIDED and tasks assigned to younger soldiers in an attempt to understand whether there are any military-strategic rationales for using children, rather than adults, in the course of hostilities.

4.1 Conditions of Participation

Whenever the use of children was deliberate, the strategy was seemingly based only on the expendability or the exploitability of children. Iranian children, for example, were sent in waves over minefields. Mozambique's RENAMO and Cambodia's Khmer Rouge in turn exploited the vulnerability of children, recognizing that a brief period of mental terror and physical abuse produced particularly fierce warriors.[1] A journalist who visited Afghan Mujahedin training schools and camps for minors observed children at their usual task of carrying water. But she also noted that, within the Mujahedin, as among the Nicaraguan contras, special treatment of children vanished when military tension mounted and exposure to combat was inevitable; discipline among child soldiers decreased, and age became irrelevant as every soldier went to the trenches.[2] In other cases, described below, children's size, agility or inconspicuousness make them particularly suitable as spies or messengers. Apart from situations in which children participate only at certain junctures for specific tasks, a young soldier will ultimately perform the same activities as an adult soldier when military necessity warrants. No effective means for preventing this outcome are apparent.

The Friends World Committee for Consultation (Quakers) has argued that, like child labour, conditions of military service for children should be investigated for possible discriminatory or exploitative practices. In a 1988 submission to the UN Working Group on Contemporary Forms of Slavery, the Quaker UN Office documented the absence of reliable information on issues such as pay scales, training, and treatment of young soldiers.[3] That

---

1 On RENAMO's process of 'socialization into violence' which included physical abuse and humiliation, punishment for displaying feelings for victims of abuse, exposure to violence, drills and exercises, forced participation in killings, and formal initiation rites, see Neil Boothby, Peter Upton, Abubacar Sultan, 'Boy Soldiers of Mozambique', *Refugee Children*, Refugee Studies Programme, Oxford, Mar. 1992, 4-5.

2 Phone interview with Alessandra Stanley, New York Times.

3 UN doc. E/CN.4/Sub.2/AC.2/1988/7 (25 May 1988). See also Mazilu, Dimitri, 'Prevention of Discrimination and Protection of Children: Human Rights and Youth: UN doc. E/CN.4/Sub.2/1992/36, 18 Jun. 1992; Working Group on Contemporary Forms of Slavery. The Recruitment of Children into Governmental Armed Forces and non-Governmental Armed Forces: UN doc. E/CN.4/Sub.2/1992/35, 25 Jan. 1992; Contemporary Forms of Slavery. The Recruitment of Children into the Armed Forces: UN doc. E/CN.4/Sub.2/1990/43, 26 Jun. 1990.

lack of data persists today,[4] and detrimental treatment is not specific to children. For example, Guatemalan highland indigenous people are poorly paid or unpaid for their mandatory participation in the civil defence patrols, regardless of age. Conversely, child soldiers are sometimes singled out for preferential treatment or enjoy social or economic benefits otherwise denied them.

Situations in which children are given specific tasks or training *because* they are children are described below, together with a few cases where children enjoy particularly enticing or even objectively valuable 'benefits'.

4.1.1 Special Education or Training for Child Soldiers

The People's Revolutionary Army (ERP), one of five FMLN factions, opened a school ('escuela de menores') in the early 1980s that offered instruction through primary level (grade 9). According to one former student who joined the ERP and entered the school in 1981 at age 9, a typical day consisted of exercise beginning at 4.45am, baths and breakfast from 6.30 to 7.30am, classes from 8.00-11.00am and an afternoon left free to memorize the day's assignment. Students successful at memorizing biographies of local heroes were asked to recite before the families of soldiers attending their child's graduation into an elite battalion, (the 'BRAZ')[5.] This former student, who had entered the school at fourth grade and studied through sixth, recalls learning about 'the other wars in Nicaragua and Cuba, about how El Salvador would soon be a new country'. He beams as he recalls his two recitals for promotions of the BRAZ and their families: 'I had a very good memory, the biographies were long - three or four full pages - and they were about things that happened even before I was born!'.[6]

Graduation to the military school followed automatically at age twelve. During the two-month military school programme students learned 'theoretical questions like how to treat the civilian population, how to accept and execute orders, to go where the Frente sent you, how to be a good revolutionary. We learned how to defend ourselves from the enemy' one former student said, 'and I didn't even know I had any enemies! I thought

---

4   Anecdotal information is fairly abundant. For example, a report from the Philippines relates the story of a peasant boy called Johnny who joined the CAFGU (paramilitary civil defence units) at age 14. The report claims that 'regular CAFGU members are given a monthly allowance of P500, but CAFGU kids like Johnny who are treated as volunteers get only a free supply of cigarettes and hard drinks which they bring to their foxholes "to battle the cold" every time they are assigned to guard the detachment.' Maritess Torres, 'Children in Combat,' in *Children of the Storm*, Children's Rehabilitation Center, Philippines (1992).

5   BRAZ = *Batallón Rafael Arce Zablah*.

6   Interview with Salvadoran ex-combatant. All interviews conducted by Ilene Cohn; names withheld at interviewees' request.

I was too young to have enemies, but there, with the Frente, I learned that yes, I had enemies'.[7]

Not all 'special training' programmes generate such fond memories as those held by some former FMLN soldiers. The Quaker United Nations Office has highlighted the RENAMO conditioning of Mozambican children through beatings and abuse, the training in 'Gonzalo Thought' forced upon Peruvian indigenous children, the meagre food and shelter conditions and the lack of teaching supplies at SPLF schools in southern Sudan, and the rigorous, even dangerous training undergone by boys in Libyan training camps.[8]

4.1.2 Specific Tasks assigned to Child Soldiers

When it came to unloading boats of arms arriving from Nicaragua in the middle of the night, one FMLN commander explained that children and elderly people, in whose nearby homes the arms were temporarily stored, were considered among the most trustworthy.[9] Though this was a temporary task for civilian children, young full-time soldiers manning FMLN checkpoints or acting as lookouts were a common sight. In 1987, Americas Watch reported that:

> There have been increased efforts by both sides to infiltrate the other to gain the best possible intelligence on their respective activities. The Armed Forces have used children as young as 13 as informers, paying them to point out suspected subversives....The FMLN has recruited children for armed military duties and support activities as messengers and pathfinders. The Americas Watch knows of cases in which boys as young as 11 years old have been used on a full-time basis as messengers, and we have seen boys who appear to be under 15 years of age armed and dressed in FMLN uniforms in the company of guerrillas.[10]

Some of the children acting as spies for the armed forces were apparently coerced to do so after having been arrested; others reportedly collaborated against the wishes of their parents or legal guardians. The FMLN responded to Americas Watch inquiries stating that the children were orphans in the FMLN's care, were accompanying armed family members, had chosen to be

---

7 Interview with Salvadoran ex-combatant.
8 Dorothea E. Woods, 'Children Bearing Military Arms', Quaker United Nations Office, Geneva, Nov.-Dec 1992.
9 Interview with ex-combatant FMLN officer.
10 *The Civilian Toll (1986-1987),* Americas Watch, 30 Aug. 1987, pp. 19, 25.

active with their parents' consent, were not combatants, or were peasant children who normally engage in adult activities at an early age.[11]

A Filipino NGO reports that '[t]he political nature of the conflict and the tactics used by the combatants have resulted in increasing recruitment of children and youth as combatants or their mobilization for war-related activities. Examples of the latter are children acting as: couriers, spies, supporters.'[12] In Uganda children served as spies, information gatherers and messengers. According to a Ugandan National Resistance Army officer: 'In the beginning, they mostly helped around the camps. With time the kids pressed; they wanted to get guns and fight for the cause. Most of the time they were refused. But then, later, some went into battle.'[13]

Little is known about the training or daily lives of young Tamil LTTE fighters; they are posted far from their homes, retain little or no contact with their families and were inaccessible during our inquiries in Sri Lanka. A Tamil administrator living in the LTTE-controlled north, who spoke on condition of anonymity, claimed to have seen the boys routinely beginning their days singing of fearlessness and the fight for their country. Some local residents said the boys receive both standard education and combat training; others claimed they only received the latter. Youth employed to run messages, distribute leaflets or perform support duties reportedly do not wear the cyanide capsules that all fighters, young and old, wear around their necks, to be taken in case of capture or in the event they are wounded and beyond rescue.

A Zimbabwean officer who fought against the Smith regime explained it simply: Children can move about freely and are not instantly suspected of spying or supplying. In guerilla warfare, children are an important link to the civilian population, whose overall support is vital. If children co-operate with insurgents, parents or entire villages can hardly do otherwise. And finally, children show a deeper sense of loyalty than can be expected from adults.[14] While that same officer stressed that children had only ever been used as civilian support, such discretion can no longer be assumed, as the brutalizing practices in Mozambique, Liberia, Cambodia and elsewhere have demonstrated only too well.

The explanations given by the FMLN or the Ugandan NRA commander do not excuse the violation of Additional Protocol II, article 4(3)(c), which

---

11   Ibid., at 60, 153.

12   *Filipino Children in Situations of Armed Conflict*, LAWASIA Human Rights Report (1989), p.16. See also Elizabeth Marcelino, 'Children at War', *Children of the Storm*, vol. 3, no.1, Children's Rehabilitation Center, Manila, July 1991-March 1992, p. 29.

13   E. Gargan, 'In Uganda, a Children's Army,' *International Herald Tribune*, 5 Aug. 1986.

14   Information provided to the Zimbabwean Red Cross as part of a survey conducted for this study.

requires the protection of children above and beyond what they, their parents or guardians may consent to. For their own protection, children should be prohibited from wearing uniforms, carrying arms, moving about with troops, or living in military bases which are legitimate military targets. But when children's realities are defined by war's causes and by-products, such as displacement, separation, loss of parents, lack of food and shelter, should we not anticipate the choice that some children will make?

4.1.3 The 'Positive' Side of Participation

Ironically, some young people perceive their own personal security to be greater inside armed opposition movements than outside, with other orphans, street children, refugees and displaced civilians.

Many of the thousands of children and youth fighting with the Ugandan National Resistance Army in the early to mid-1980s had been driven from their homes and lost their families to rampaging government troops. They sought, or were picked up and adopted by the NRA, where they found a 'home', stability, loyalty, discipline, empowerment and the prospect of promotion, respect and pride. 'And the commanders themselves, for all their tough military exteriors, [were] very paternalistic to "their boys", keeping a close eye on their well-being...The boy soldiers [were] not...brutalized...They [had] been tutored for hours each day by their "political commissars" on the importance not of Marx or Mao but of discipline and honesty, and above all, respect for the rights of ordinary citizens.'[15] As noted above,[16] much the same scenario unfolded in El Salvador. Not all young soldiers are 'used' or 'victimized' by older soldiers or commanders; most will certainly have suffered, but often due to circumstances pre-dating and more complex then their membership or role in an armed group.

In 1983, after talking with Irish, Palestinian, and Israeli 'children of war', Roger Rosenblatt considered whether a state of war offered anything good for children. He found that war gave child participants a mission in life, order, hierarchy, physical fitness, a sense of importance, of being essential to both a particular goal and an abstract idea. He found that Palestinian children felt needed, both spiritually and practically, and they readily responded to the needs of others. Friendships were enhanced by a state of war and the institutions of an army provided stability for its members.

---

15 Peter Godwin, 'The Boys' Own Army,' *The Times*, London, 27 Apr. 1986, at 42A.
16 See section 2.1.3.

> Children, who are natural conservatives, will make a family of such an institution; this is their territory, their place in the order of things....Armies like the PLO and the IRA may hold a particular appeal for children, because they are both wild and conservative simultaneously, thus allowing more excitement within their stability than do the standing armed forces of an established power. They also enforce ideologies, as standing armies rarely do. A kid fighting with a bunch of rebels is far more apt to know why he is doing it than a recruit of a national guard. Beside all this there is even a psychoanalytic theory that holds that a state of war may be beneficial for the subconscious in that it relieves it of self-contempt....Finally, a war allows boys to look like men. This seems a shallow benefit, but it is no small thing for a teenage boy to have something that yanks him out of his social floundering and places him, unlaughed at, in the company of heroes.[17]

Rosenblatt concluded that war cannot be valuable, for it replaces freedom of thought and opinion with one ideology, and because war's final purpose is to create chaos and ruin, despite its superficial emphasis on order and discipline. War is a moral lie, he says, but a lie we all share; 'war is the way the world progresses.'[18]

4.2   Short-term and Long-term Consequences of Participation

Because child combatants' experiences are as varied as their cultures and the conflicts themselves, the short or long-term consequences of participation cannot be neatly charted or summarized.

Information is scarce because in situations of conflict or strife, child and young participants are often inaccessible for other than media purposes.[19] Local people can be at risk if they try to reach these children, and international agencies often do not try, arguing that such involvement would be politically harmful or is prohibited by the host government. Some consequences of participation manifest themselves during hostilities, however, and can be monitored even in war-time.

The following sections follow no strict categorization, but deal with

17   Roger Rosenblatt, *Children of War,* Anchor Press/Doubleday, New York, 1983, p. 101.
18   Ibid., at 204.
19   In the course of this study, Ilene Cohn visited Liberia, Sri Lanka, El Salvador, Guatemala, Israel and the occupied territories. In Liberia and Sri Lanka, time and/or practical constraints made it impossible personally to assess the conditions of the fighting, and in neither place were NGOs working directly with child combatants. Reports from the field indicate much the same is true in the Philippines, southern Sudan, Somalia, Afghanistan and Peru.

commonly occurring issues affecting large numbers of child soldiers. Within the case studies presented below, local responses are described. Chapter 5 describes the legal obligations to respond to the issues raised below, and presents suggestions for responsive programme and policy initiatives at the local, regional and international levels.

4.2.1 Detention

The capture or detention of members of an armed group or opposition force occurs in all conflicts. In some cases, contrary to international humanitarian law, the captors kill all prisoners, in others those captured or at risk of being captured commit suicide as a matter of policy.[20] Sometimes, an armed group grants international monitors access to the detained and allows scrutiny of its treatment of detainees; at other times, no access is granted and it is impossible even to verify whether a presumed detainee is alive.[21]

The applicable international legal norms vary, depending on the conflict type, and the level of protection due to children may also vary, depending on age. Prisoner of war (POW) status flows from combatant status, which in turn is only accorded in international armed conflicts. If, contrary to international law, children under 15 years participate directly in hostilities and are captured, Additional Protocol I, article 77(3) provides for their special protection, whether or not they have combatant status. During violent strife or internal armed conflict a child, like an adult, might be detained for reasons of suspected participation in 'terrorist or subversive activities', actual participation in hostilities, or even desertion from the armed forces or an armed group. In strife situations not covered by international humanitarian law, detainees are subject to national penal law, which in turn may be governed by minimum obligations and standards with respect to human rights. National laws and procedures should at least provide the guarantees laid down in *Common Article 3* of the Geneva Conventions, articles 37 and 40 of the Convention on the Rights of the Child, and the juvenile justice standards endorsed by the United Nations.[22]

---

20   It has been reported that the Sri Lankan LTTE killed all those it captured. Thousands of disappearances following detention have been attributed to the Sri Lankan army, security forces, police and paramilitary groups. See *Report on a Visit to Sri Lanka by three members of the Working Group on Enforced or Involuntary Disappearances* (7-18 October 1991), UN doc. E/CN.4/1992/18/Add.1 (8 Jan. 1992), at 20-3. LTTE fighters, including children, reportedly wear cyanide capsules around their necks to prevent their being captured alive and a number have taken the capsules both before and after capture.

21   The FMLN in El Salvador declared adherence to Protocol II and submitted to Americas Watch scrutiny of its fair trial procedures for detainees; see *Violation of Fair Trial Guarantees by the FMLN's Ad Hoc Courts*, Americas Watch, Washington D.C., May 1990. On the other hand, even the ICRC has no access to Tamils presumed detained by the LTTE in the northern Jaffna province.

22   For further detail, see Chapter 5 below.

Such is not always the case, however, and juvenile justice procedures call for further investigation and reform. Major practical problems also arise regarding the capacity or willingness of both governmental and non-governmental armed entities to comply with national and international law standards governing the treatment of detainees.

4.2.1.1 Child Prisoners of War (POWs) and Captured Child Soldiers: Iranians and Ethiopians

Tens of thousands of Iranians were held in POW camps in Iraq, including several hundred children. Newspaper accounts describing the conditions of detention reported no physical abuse; on the contrary, healthy child POWs were excellent propaganda for the Iraqis, who brought them out for journalists, to answer questions about recruitment, training and battle experiences in the Iranian armed forces. So it was that the world learned of the thousands of Iranian children enticed or coerced to the frontline, armed with makeshift rifles, a dose of 'martyr's syrup', and the keys to paradise around their necks.[23] Several hundred who survived their role as human mine-sweepers spent years in Iraqi POW camps.

Iraq's attempts to return Iranian child POWs were rebuffed by the Khomeini government, which was said to prefer martyrs to heroes. 'In any case, outsiders fear[ed] with good reason that children sent back [in 1984] would [have been] abused for allowing themselves to be captured, accused of having been brainwashed and turned traitor...It would [have been] impolitic to send them to a non-Moslem country. Ayatollah Khomeini would [have said] that Iraq was selling Iran's children to the infidel.'[24]

In spite of Iraqi propaganda efforts and media reports of over 24,000 Iranian soldiers killed in a matter of hours in just one battle, there was very little international outrage. As a leader of Denmark's peace movement said, 'We can't identify with it. It was easy to identify with brave little Vietnamese fighting a superpower, or with Afghans.' Or in other words, if 'you can't tell the white hats from the black hats, it doesn't matter how many are killed.'[25] One commentator suggested that if a negotiated solution could not be achieved, the US might have pressured Pakistan to accept the children POWs, thereby removing them from the battle zones.[26] It did not happen, however, and the POWs sat where they were until after the end of the war.

---

23   See Henry Kamm, 'Iraq Displays Teenagers Held as Prisoners of War.' *The New York Times*, 8 Mar. 1984; David B. Ottaway, 'Child POWs: Captured Young Iranians Languish in Iraqi Prison,' *Washington Post*, 7 Jul. 1984. Also, Louyot, Alain, *Les Gosses de Guerre*, Paris, 1989, chapter 2.

24   Flora Lewis, 'A Decent Respect...,' *The New York Times*, 26 Apr. 1984.

25   Ibid.

26   Ibid.

International NGOs meanwhile worked to improve the conditions of detention. Under the Third Geneva Convention, Iraq was bound only to encourage educational activities for POWs, but Defence for Children International and Terre des Hommes (both based in Switzerland) stepped in to offer educational and training opportunities to Iranian POWs under age 18.[27] The children's attitudes and wishes were considered and the choice of courses and teachers was greatly influenced by their opinions, as well as by specific security, legal and cultural considerations.

In the late 1980s hundreds of Ethiopian youth under 18, who had been forcibly recruited by the Ethiopian armed forces, were captured by the EPLF.[28] Like the Iranian boys, they spent years in the camps; and like the Iranian government, the Ethiopian government showed no interest in the fate of its soldiers once captured. Unlike the Iranians, however, they did not benefit from POW status under the Third Geneva Convention, since the war was not characterised as an international armed conflict. When the Mengistu regime was overthrown in May 1991, the ICRC attempted to trace the families of unaccompanied ex-child soldiers and other children who were now released. But the families themselves often showed no interest in welcoming back their children, who in turn felt they were better off in the orphanages. A commission was reportedly set up to assist with the reintegration of former soldiers, including youth, into both rural and urban civilian life.

No projects similar to that set up for Iranian child POWs by international NGOs seem to have been implemented for captured Ethiopian children, and the ICRC was unable even to register or visit them. We are not aware of any psychosocial research or programme information on these or any other child combatants who have been detained over long periods of time.

4.2.1.2 Due Process for Children: Palestinians in the Israeli Occupied Territories

The situation in the territories occupied by Israel for the last twenty-six years raises problematic legal issues, in addition to the human issues emerging from the widespread violence which involves considerable numbers of Palestinian children and youth. The international community and the ICRC consider that the Fourth Geneva Convention applies to the occupied territories, limiting Israel's freedom of action with respect to the civilian population. Israel has always resisted the application of legal

27　See Defence for Children International, informal reports: 'Report on a Mission to Iraq: Evaluation of Educational Assistance Possibilities to Iranian Child-Soldiers in Prisoner-of-War Camps in Iraq (9-15 Dec. 1983)'; also 'Report on Second Mission to Iraq (25-29 May 1984)'.

28　T.R. Lansner, 'In Ethiopia, a P.O.W. at 15,' *The New York Times*, 15 Oct. 1989.

standards, including now the Convention on the Rights of the Child. The facts, however, are sufficiently compelling to require both a legal assessment of Israeli conduct, and the implementation of effective programmes for the maintenance of international standards and the protection of children and youth.

Palestinian youth detained in the occupied territories in connection with *intifada* violence lack sufficient legal protection and a whole host of abuses flowing from the detention have been reported: abusive interrogation procedures,[29] psychological trauma,[30] inadequate detention facilities, disregard of visiting rights, lack of explanation of procedures to detainees and their families. Matters are further complicated by the number of detainees held for long periods,[31] the absence of clear international guidelines on detention, the confinement of protected persons in a situation of occupation lasting over decades, and the variety of law and social institutions in Gaza, the West Bank and East Jerusalem. Not surprisingly, a number of highly qualified Palestinian, Israeli, and international human rights monitors have decried the treatment of Palestinian minor detainees ever since mass arrests began in early 1988.[32]

Both Israeli and Palestinian NGOs have challenged deficient provision of specific due process guarantees, provided legal representation for detained minors, taken complaints through the Israeli court system, and demanded fairer legislation and consistent implementation of existing law, and more extensive public scrutiny and investigation of the treatment of

29 See for example, *The Interrogation of Palestinians during the Intifada: Follow-up to March 1991 B'Tselem Report*, B'Tselem (the Israeli Information Center for Human Rights in the Occupied Territories), Jerusalem, Mar. 1992; *Israel's Use of Shock Torture in the Interrogation of Palestinian Detainees* PHRIC, Jerusalem, 2nd ed., Jul. 1992.

30 See for example, Charles Greenbaum, 'Police Violence Against Minors - Psychological Aspects,' in *Violence against Minors in Detention,* B'Tselem Information Sheet: Update June-July 1990, at 5; Palestinian children's accounts of psychological abuse in detention, including threats of violence, 'good cop/bad cop' police techniques, sleep deprivation and humiliation, in 'The Arrest, Detention and Physical Abuse of Palestinian Children' in *From the Field*, Palestinian Human Rights Information Center (PHRIC), Jerusalem, monthly report, August/September 1991.

31 ICRC reported a total of 932 youth under age 18 in detention at 21 Sept. 1992. This includes detainees in all military detention centres, police stations and prisons, registered and being visited by the ICRC.

32 See for example, 'Israeli Interrogation Methods Under Fire After Death of Detained Palestinian', Middle East Watch Bulletin, Vol. 4, Issue 6, Mar. 1992; 'The Arrest, Detention and Physical Abuse of Palestinian Children,' in *From the Field*, Palestinian Human Rights Information Center, Jerusalem (August-September 1991); *Violence Against Minors in Police Detention*, B'Tselem Information Sheet: Update June-July 1990; Marcia Kretzmer, 'Not a Minor Problem,' *The Jerusalem Post*, 1 Jun. 1989, page 7; Anne E. Nixon, *The Status of Palestinian Children during the Uprising in the Occupied Territories,* Rädda Barnen (1990).

minors within the justice system.[33] Still, outside East Jerusalem there is no juvenile justice system for Palestinian youth; rights monitors lack access to detention facilities, so that information is incomplete, and the Israeli Defence Forces are said to enjoy *de facto* impunity for abuses against those detained.

Defence for Children International, which has both Israeli and Palestinian branches, began offering legal counsel to detained youth in March 1992. By November 1992, their lawyer in the West Bank had taken on forty-six cases of juveniles accused of stone throwing, tire burning, membership in illegal organizations, and attempted stabbing or murder. Her clients were mainly 16-17 year olds, with a number of 15-16 year olds, and the youngest being 14. She and several other Israeli and Palestinian lawyers identified the following additional rights violations and obstacles to a fair and prompt trial: beating under interrogation, translation problems, lack of access by lawyers, bail beyond the reach of poorer families, delays and postponements, inconsistent sentencing patterns, and sub-standard conditions of detention.[34]

The situation is only marginally better for Palestinians in East Jerusalem, where Israeli law applies. There are too few Arab parole officers to cope with the many *intifada* youth charged, for example, with arson and endangering life in motor vehicles (that is, stoning cars). Bail is set beyond the financial capacity of most parents and older youth are generally detained without bail from indictment through to sentencing. Prison conditions are overcrowded, cold and dirty. Sentencing patterns for Jewish as opposed to Palestinian minors are inconsistent, a number of reports cite violent interrogation of minors and police threats of violence against the families of minor detainees, and the investigation of police violence is sluggish, at best.[35] Detainees are kept out of school and away from their families, increasing the incentive for them to 'confess'.

---

33 Such pressure has reportedly led to a reduction in the numbers of children under age 13 detained by the authorities; see 'The Arrest, Detention and Physical Abuse of Palestinian Children' in *From the Field*, Palestinian Human Rights Information Center, monthly report, August/September 1991, p.1. The 'Hotline for Victims of Violence', formed in summer 1988, takes individual cases of rights violations in Israel and the occupied territories, many of which deal with lack of notification to families regarding the whereabouts of detained persons; see 'The Activities of "Hotline: Center for the Defense of the Individual"',' *Information Sheet*, Aug. 1991, B'Tselem, Jerusalem.

34 Marcia Kretzmer, 'Overcrowded, unsanitary jail life for youths,' *The Jerusalem Post*, 26 Jul. 1989.

35 *Violence against Minors in Police Detention*, Information Sheet: Update June-July 1990, B'Tselem (the Israeli Information Center for Human Rights in the Occupied Territories), pp. 29-30.

4.2.1.3 Criminal Responsibility under National Legislation:
The Case of Peru

In Peru, the age of criminal responsibility has been lowered, supposedly to facilitate the conviction of minors between 15 and 18 years for the crime of terrorism.[36] Although presented as a necessary component in the battle against terrorism, the new decree has been criticized as ineffective and a facile attempt to elicit public support. Because *Sendero Luminoso* does appear to recruit those under 15 the new decree will not stop terrorism perpetrated by children. The major effect of the new decree will be to reduce the legal protection of 15-18 year olds, thereby increasing the likelihood of police harassment. In September 1991 Americas Watch asserted that torture was a frequent practice against those detained on suspicion of terrorism, that the courts were ineffective in dealing with such complaints, and that at the time the ICRC was 'not given access to the detainees immediately after arrest but only after preventive detention, which in terrorism cases can last up to 15 days.'[37] The greatest danger of mistreatment is in the initial period of detention and Americas Watch recommended that the ICRC be granted access within 24 hours.[38] Cramped prison conditions and untrained prison staff will add to the deteriorating situation.[39] Some commentators have suggested that the State would contribute more to reducing youth participation in terrorist acts by rebuilding the school system and providing employment opportunities.[40]

Looking at the facts, there can be little doubt that the situation in Peru is one to which *Common Article 3* applies, necessitating minimum standards of humane treatment and respect for dignity. But Peru has also ratified the Convention on the Rights of the Child, article 37 of which both confirms these basic rules and prohibits unlawful or arbitrary arrest and detention. Detention in the case of children under eighteen is a 'measure of last resort', to be used for the shortest appropriate period of time, whereas every detained child is to have 'prompt access' to legal assistance and to be able to challenge the legality of the detention before an independent and impartial authority. National legislation and practice clearly need to be assessed against applicable international obligations and standards,

---

36   Decreto-Ley 25564, 20 de Junio 1992, modifying article 20(2) of the Penal Code.

37   *Into the Quagmire: Human Rights and U.S. Policy in Peru*, Americas Watch, Sept. 1991, p.17.

38   Ibid.

39   Rafael Leon, 'D.L. 25564: Penalizacion de Menores, Absurdo sin Maquillaje', *Area Chica*, Rädda Barnen, Aug. 1992.

40   Carlos Ivan Degregori, Javier de Belaunde, 'Opinion', *Area Chica*, Rädda Barnen, Aug. 1992.

including those formally accepted by Peru as well as those deriving from customary international law.

4.2.1.4 Forcibly recruited Minors charged with Desertion: The Case of El Salvador

When human rights observers and legal officers of the United Nations Observer Mission in El Salvador (ONUSAL) investigated the provision of due process guarantees, they found a number of minors detained for desertion. Until mid-1992 the secondary legislation prescribed by the Constitution to regulate recruitment in El Salvador had never been adopted.[41] A military decree, signed by the Vice-Minister of Defence in January 1991, exempted males under eighteen from mandatory service.[42] Except for a very small number who had joined voluntarily as minors, all those held for desertion in one particular jail had been forcibly recruited. Often, they had escaped wearing their uniforms or carrying backpacks and arms. Before heading home, some buried what they had, while others kept what they were carrying, but in either case theft charges were added to the charge of desertion. The international law division of the Ministry of Defence agreed in principle that an illegally recruited, under-age minor could not commit the crime of desertion, but military legal procedure ignored the age factor. In addition, the legal protection was inadequate. During seven months or so of incarceration, the detainees attempted to produce their birth certificates to prove their under-age status, but their efforts were disregarded, and no legal representation was provided.

The deficiencies in national legal protection in this situation, to which Additional Protocol II applied, can be appreciated when national process and practice are compared with the special protection due to children under article 4, or with article 37 of the Convention on the Rights of the Child, also ratified by El Salvador. As a practical matter, the effective protection of detainees in such situations will only improve when institutions like the human rights ombudsman or the public defender's offices are established or strengthened, and legal aid NGOs can take up such cases without fear of reprisal.

4.2.2 Psychosocial Consequences of Participation

Under the Convention on the Rights of the Child, every child is entitled to

41   Article 215 of El Salvador's Constitution (1983) establishes mandatory military service for those between 18-30 years old. The same article also provides that secondary legislation will regulate the recruitment of Salvadorans 'in case of necessity'.

42   'Instructivo para Regular la Concesion de Exhoneraciones del Servicio Militar Obligatorio', para. III(a)(2), Ministerio de Defensa y de Seguridad Publica, 23 Enero 1991.

receive such 'protection and care as is necessary for his or her well-being' and States parties are obliged to 'ensure to the maximum extent possible the survival and development of the child'. Moreover, States are obliged to protect children from all forms of mental violence or abuse and to strive to ensure that victims of armed conflict have access to rehabilitative care.[43]

Any one child's story will include a set of factors that may have influenced the nature and degree of his or her involvement in the hostilities. That history, up-dated to include the experience of participation in an armed conflict, can produce different psychosocial consequences for different children. Their pre- and post-war social and economic conditions will vary, as will their war-related experiences; they will subjectively process these differently, so that even similar experiences may affect children in very distinct ways. They may return home heroes or villains, to loving families and receptive communities; or they may have no home, no family and no identity beyond that of combatant.

Positive consequences can also result. Inside an armed group or force a child may find more social support or empowerment, or the validation and respect of family, teachers and peers, emerging more secure and with increased prosocial tendencies. Some have cited heightened national identity as a 'benefit' of armed conflict, claiming that this buffers some children from the otherwise deleterious effects of conflict. Others fear that heightened national or ethnic identity, which can imply increased resentment against an opposing nation or group, can only be detrimental to reconciliation and peace in the long run.

Many of the issues discussed in this chapter — detention, physical injury, disciplinary problems, breakdown of family structure — may contribute to or represent psychosocial symptoms or adaptational problems in child participants. The psychosocial consequences in ex-combatant children can be short-term and long-term, and a child soldier suffering psychosocial symptoms while still involved in fighting might even pose a particular danger to others.

The following pages review the research and observations of experts, describing traumatic experiences of child soldiers proven or believed to be associated with negative or positive psychosocial outcomes.

4.2.2.1 Traumatic experiences and psychosocial outcomes

Execution and experience of violent acts. Even while children victims of war have been able, with assistance, to recover a reasonable level of psychosocial well-being, the recuperative powers of children who have

43   Arts. 3(2), 6(2), 19, 39.

themselves perpetrated violence is greatly diminished.

> After a month in a camp in Thailand, one 15-year-old who had been a
> Khmer Rouge cadre for four years began hearing two voices 'arguing with
> each other inside my head.' The first was a voice of a Khmer Rouge leader
> who was angry because the boy deserted; the second, that of a Buddhist
> priest who 'says even when I die I will be punished for what I've done.'
> Another 13-year-old Khmer Rouge saw visions in which the intestines of
> one of his victims turned into snakes that then began to strangle him. In
> clinical sessions with other former child soldiers from Guatemala,
> Ethiopia and elsewhere, I also found that their psychological turmoil
> became most acute after they laid down their guns and attempted to
> re-enter civilian communities. It was their rediscovery of killing as a moral
> transgression that seemed to prompt their mental suffering.[44]

The last point was equally true of Mozambican children undergoing a
psychosocial rehabilitation programme after escaping from the rebel forces
that had forced them to commit atrocities. A 10-year-old who had been
abducted by RENAMO, subjected to brutal training and ultimately forced to
kill civilians and soldiers before escaping and finding refuge in a Maputo
orphanage, was found to be suspicious of adults and suffering from
'flashbacks in which events from the past would come flooding back at
unexpected moments to haunt him.'[45] The story is typical of thousands of
Mozambican youth.

A preliminary survey by the Liberian Opportunities Industrialization
Center (LOIC) in 1991 revealed widespread exposure to violence and death
and the commission of barbarous acts. Similar experiences can be predicted
in Somalia, Cambodia, and Bosnia, among others.

Childhood exposure to chronic fear and anxiety. Although the bulk of
existing research explores the psychosocial impact of domestic violence
and/or war on children, some psychologists suggest a connection between
exposure to chronic fear and anxiety as children and susceptibility to later
recruitment into terrorist or armed groups. In Northern Ireland, for example,
it has been suggested that Catholic children, who exhibit more signs of stress
than Protestant children, may join the IRA as an outlet for anger, a way of
getting revenge on those perceived to have caused them so much pain.[46] No

44   Neil Boothby, 'The New Face of War', unpublished paper, abstracted from War and Refugee
Children, Oxford University Press.
45   Neil Boothby, 'Living in the War Zone,' *World Refugee Survey - 1989 in Review*, pp.40-2.
46   Daniel Goleman, 'Terror's Children: Mending Mental Wounds,' *The New York Times*,
24 Feb. 1987, C1, C12.

systematic study appears to have been conducted into the relationship between the way children cope with or process violence as young victims and their propensity for later joining armed groups. Such research could well help in developing interventions that might avert youth participation at an earlier stage.

The desire for revenge. Fear and the desire for revenge, most often directly related to having witnessed violent acts and the killing of family members or loved ones, motivated thousands of children to join the Ugandan NRA. Kabanda was nine when he watched UNLA soldiers kill his parents:

> Kabanda has strong feelings. 'The men who kill my mother, they make me angry. Me, I decide to go in the army. Me, I decide to beat them. If I find them, I kill.'.... On February 3rd [1986], 13-year-old Stephen Ogwang witnessed UNLA soldiers rage through his village, massacring more than a dozen people....'I know these people they killed. This one, when I would come home from school and I be hungry, he would give me food. Now I will remember. Those men who killed my friend, they should be killed.' The NRA is taking seriously the task of eradicating the desire for revenge. They are a well-disciplined force, and raping, looting and killing - the hallmarks of the UNLA - are not tolerated. Commander Edwin Kamoomo is in the 11th Battalion, and there are five children in his company, the youngest being 11 years old. 'If they have bad intentions towards those who killed their families, the only thing to do is to discourage them, to tell them how things should be handled. As NRA is in power now, everyone who did bad will be taken to court and the court will decide how to deal with him.'[47]

In debating whether military or civilian education was more suitable for Ugandan child soldiers after the war, advocates for the latter argued that the children's strong desire for revenge might make them a volatile element within the military, should the new government fall short of their hopes or expectations. No longitudinal studies have described the mental health of Ugandan child soldiers in later years. Even if the children's education was later provided by the military, the fact that Ugandan children sought out, were protected by and grew loyal to the NRA, joined with the fact that the NRA was victorious and highly disciplined, might shift the probabilities in

---

47   Lindsey Hilsum, 'Not too small to kill', *Children First*, (The magazine of UNICEF/UK), Autumn 1986, pp. 16-18.

favour of these children overcoming their desire for revenge and integrating successfully into the community.

Just as the root causes of a conflict offer a starting point for understanding the traumatic experiences that influence some children to join armed groups, the larger processes by which a conflict is resolved are also relevant to understanding how child soldiers will come to grips with their personal war experiences. The case of Uganda can be contrasted with that of El Salvador, Sri Lanka, the Israeli occupied territories, or Somalia. Where a negotiated solution has or will probably compel compromises on all sides, such as amnesties, children who participated for revenge or other specific reasons might feel betrayed or frustrated. Further research is needed on the reintegration into civil society of youth whose specific motives for taking up arms were or were not addressed in the resolution of the conflict.

Fear of retribution and related feelings of guilt. The fear of rejection or the danger of physical or legal retribution for acts committed during conflict can be a subjective reaction or an objective reality. Sometimes families or communities do reject former child soldiers, either because they have committed serious abuses or because the family or community fears violent retribution for the acts of the child soldier. Fear of being found-out can lead participants to change their names or alter their personal histories, sometimes to such an extent over so much time, that one wonders how they perceive or might eventually retrieve their own identities.

NGO and international organization staff interviewed in Liberia in October 1992 anticipated high levels of popular resentment towards former combatants, given the atrocities they are known to have committed. Some believed families would reject children associated with such events, for fear of repercussions by those seeking revenge. A general amnesty had been offered by the interim government in Monrovia, but fear of retribution in a society where people are said to 'know who is who, and who did what' may outweigh its attraction. Moreover, the fear of rejection and the lack of material benefits may act as a deterrent to demobilization. Others were optimistic about the population's capacity to forgive and reconcile, however, and had even begun implementing programmes to facilitate psychological healing and reconciliation.

Relief workers in Mozambique anticipated a difficult reconciliation process, but recent reports show that such fears are now greatly diminished. For some time, an amnesty has been granted to those willing to turn in their arms. A cease-fire was signed in October 1992 and by February 1993 government troops and RENAMO fighters were reportedly exchanging polite greetings as they passed on the road. Combatants interviewed by journalists all predicted an easy reconciliation.[48]

Moral breakdown. Research is inconclusive as to the likelihood of moral breakdown among children who actively participate in political violence and armed conflict. Neil Boothby has found that children's social and moral concepts have proven quite resilient in Northern Ireland, which he links to the persisting strength of family bonds and religious values. In other cases, however, 'a kind of stunted moral development' has been observed among child participants, for example, in 'political conflicts in which concern for heritage and nation has become militarized, and participation "in the struggle" is elevated to a "rite of passage".'[49]

Among a sample of Mozambican boys, researchers found that the length of time spent in RENAMO base camps, rather than direct involvement in violence, was a factor in their later capacity to act upon traditional concepts of right and wrong. Those who had spent under six months in the camps defined themselves as victims of RENAMO, whereas those who had spent between one and two years identified themselves as members. This latter group overcame their distrust of adults, aggressive feelings and behaviours much more slowly than the former group, and it was only after three months in a rehabilitation centre that they showed any remorse for previous acts of violence or anxiety connected to reminders of other traumatic events.[50]

Political awareness and group identity. The youth at the core of the 1987 Palestinian uprising had already been extensively exposed to a range of traumatic experiences, including humiliation of themselves or their parents by the security forces, detention,[51] tear gas, physical injury, restricted freedom of movement, and denial of national identity. In the early stages, Palestinian experts acknowledged that teenagers were assuming a most active role, and noted a mixture of positive and negative mental health outcomes as a result. 'They are in the limelight and they are showing signs

48   Bill Keller, 'Mozambique's Outlook Brightens as Truce Holds and Drought Ends,' *The New York Times*, 22 Feb. 1993, A1, A6. This report suggested that fatalism, southern African tradition, a talent for postponing vengeance, or fatigue might explain the lack of vengefulness observed among Mozambicans.

49   Neil Boothby, 'Working in the War Zone: A Look at Psychological Theory and Practice from the Field,' *Mind & Human Interaction*, vol.2, no.2, Virginia, 1990, p. 33. Rona Fields, a psychologist, has suggested that children in Northern Ireland may not be so resilient as local experts had claimed: 'They reach a level of moral development where they believe that the only way to right a wrong is through revenge and violence.' See 'Living in a World of Terror', *Newsweek*, 19 Mar. 1984, p. 23.

50   Above, note 49.

51   See Ahmad Baker, 'The Psychosocial Effects of Mistreatment During Detention on Palestinian Youth,' in *Children Imprisoned*, The DataBase Project on Palestinian Human Rights, Jerusalem (1989).

of rebellion. Because they see their parents humiliated they despise them and call them cowards. Some are becoming withdrawn and uncommunicative. Others violent.'[52] But even those Palestinians portrayed as young leaders of the struggle, volunteers with nothing to lose, highly politicized youth, can suffer negative consequences of participation. Dr. Eyad El Sarraj, a Gaza psychiatrist, refers to the hidden *intifada*, which instills youth with fear, causing a range of psychosocial disorders.[53]

Researchers at the Gaza Community Mental Health Center, run by Dr. El-Sarraj, have studied children from age 15 to 18, 99% of whom have been active *intifada* participants. Broken bones were the most frequent traumatic experience, PTSD (post-traumatic stress disorder) was prevalent along with nightmares, sleep disorders and avoidance behaviours. Ahmad Baker, a Palestinian psychologist, studied a sample of 796 children in the occupied territories in 1989 and found that in this 'unique case in which children and youth are active participants in the conflict rather than passive recipients of its traumatic nature.... [Palestinian youth exhibited] elevated self-esteem despite the high percentage of reported depression symptoms..,' and are shielded from developing pathological symptoms.[54] He noted a prevalence of disobedience and a tendency to fight and disturb others, but was unable to conclude that these were brought on by the *intifada*.

Cairo Arafat, an Arab-American clinical psychologist, has noted that 'the *intifada* is having a dual impact on [Palestinian children's] psyches: building a strong sense of Palestinian identity while at the same time creating a heritage of fear and hostility toward Israelis.'[55] The fact that strong national identity formation, highly valued among Palestinians, is fostered by actions predicated on a hatred of the 'other' may well pose significant hurdles for mental health projects—and peace—over the long-term. This is especially so where other identity-formation role models, such as parents or traditional authority figures, have lost legitimacy. 'There is a new value in Palestinian society: taking part in the uprising. Youngsters are often more radical than their parents and by acting independently, they have revolutionized the traditional structure of the family.' Sons accuse fathers of not doing enough for the uprising, they have seen their fathers humiliated at the hands of Israeli security forces or civil administration officials, and are no longer 'willing to sacrifice their national aspirations,

52 Statement of Dr. Eyad El-Sarraj, Gaza psychiatrist, quoted by Caroline Moorehead, 'Territory where Fear Starts from Birth', *The Independent*, 20 Nov. 1989.
53 G. Usher, 'Children of Palestine', *Race and Class*, vol. 32, no.4, April-June 1991, p.5.
54 Ahmad M. Baker, 'The Impact of the Intifada on the Mental Health of Palestinian Children Living in the Occupied Territories,' unpublished paper, Birzeit, West Bank, 1989.
55 Glenn Frankel, 'Palestinian Youth See Life as War,' *The Washington Post*, 1 Jul. 1989.

even if this goes against the will of their parents'.[56] Parents on the other hand send mixed messages to their children: they fear for their lives yet acknowledge that they cannot keep their children from going outside; they worry about injuries, yet the children sense their parents' pride in their involvement.

4.2.3 Physical Injury

Like adults, child soldiers suffer all manner of physical injury. Whether they face different types of injury because of the different tasks assigned to younger soldiers, and whether different rehabilitation techniques for youth are warranted, proved next to impossible to determine: Either injuries to children or injuries to combatants are reported, but without differentiating between child soldiers and others, while obvious practical difficulties prevent accurate counts of casualties among non-governmental entities. Anecdotal information is also of uncertain value; for example, the Liberian National Reconciliation Commission reported in October 1992 that young former members of Charles Taylor's troops showed a high incidence of hernias, presumably from carrying weapons too heavy for their small size, and eye injuries, possibly due to weapons backfiring.

Organizations and researchers reporting on *intifada*-related injuries and deaths among minors in the occupied territories do not distinguish participants in, and victims of, the clashes. An extensive study of Palestinian children found only that slightly more than a quarter of the children killed by gunfire during the first two years of uprising were participating in stone-throwing.[57] In such a fluid and volatile situation it is hard to verify whether those killed were actively involved.

Of the 2,301 FMLN combatants handicapped during the war who returned to civilian life over the course of 1992, 106 (4.6%) were between eleven and seventeen years old. A much higher percentage was injured years ago, when they too were minors, and have since been *hors de combat*. What types of injuries they suffered, or whether certain types of injury were more prevalent among children, cannot be determined.

4.2.4 The Impact of Participation on Education: Lost School Time

Although many children are denied access to education even in peace time, the child soldier risks foregoing educational opportunities entirely, with the possible exception of those scant opportunities to study offered by some

---

56   Philip Veerman, 'Challenge to our Image of Childhood,' *The Jerusalem Post*, 24 Sept. 1989.
57   Anne E. Nixon, *The Status of Palestinian Children during the Uprising in the Occupied Territories,* vol.1, part 1, p.5, Rädda Barnen, 1990.

armed groups. A preliminary survey of young FMLN combatants in the Guazapa area, conducted in 1992, showed that most were below the educational level normal for their age groups. Twenty-two percent of all combatants in the area were under 18 years old, and 32% of those were girls. The majority expressed interest in furthering their education after their demobilization.

In the Israeli occupied territories the education of Palestinian youth suffers for two reasons: either the uprising leadership imposes strike days or encourages the participation of students in *intifada*-related episodes during school hours; or security forces order the schools closed for 'security reasons'.[58] The Israeli Ministry of Justice has claimed that

> ...schools in the areas have become centres for PLO and extremist Islamic activity and meeting places for students actively involved in intifada violence. In fact, at times the schools have become recruitment centres for willing or unwilling participants. PLO extremists have entered classrooms and forced pupils out into the streets to participate in riots...As a result, the Israeli government has temporarily closed schools which have ceased to act as centres for education.[59]

On numerous occasions, blanket West Bank school closures were imposed by the security forces, thus punishing far more students than those at the specific schools that were focal points for clashes with security forces. The authorities never established that the hundreds of other pupils in schools directly affected by closures ever posed a security risk. Moreover, school closures in the West Bank did not reduce the number of clashes. Indeed, 'in the Gaza Strip, where schools remained open and the system functioned normally, there was no indication that this triggered or intensified clashes with the security forces.'[60]

Not only has the punishment failed to affect the level of violence, but according to an Israeli clinical psychologist the school closures, which affect huge numbers of adolescents passing through a turbulent emotional and psychological stage in their lives, may even foment violence by driving

58   See *Israel's War against Education in the Occupied West Bank: A Penalty for the Future*, Al Haq, Law in the Service of Man, Ramallah, November 1988.

59   'Children as Participants in the Intifada', Ministry of Justice, Jerusalem, 26 November 1989.

60   *Closure of Schools and Other Setbacks to the Education System in the Occupied Territories*, Information Sheet: Update September-October 1990, B'tselem - The Israeli Information Center for Human Rights in the Occupied Territories, Jerusalem, p.12.

increased numbers of frustrated youth to alternative organizational structures such as militant or combative groups.[61]

4.2.5 Collateral Consequences affecting Families or Society
Families, communities, and entire societies have suffered the repercussions of the participation of children or youth in armed groups or forces.

Collective punishment. Examples of collective punishments include the house demolitions[62] and sealings, curfews, mass arrests and mass deportations of Palestinians in the occupied territories, the forced displacement of approximately one million persons and exodus of some 500,000 persons from El Salvador in the 1980s as a result of army efforts to 'drain the fish from the sea', army roadblocks that prohibited the passage of food to certain communities in El Salvador suspected of harbouring FMLN troops, the scorched earth and psychological warfare policies of the Guatemalan military that targeted entire indigenous ethnic groups in the 1980s, wiping hundreds of towns entirely off the map. In Peru entire families or communities have been massacred, dozens of individuals have been assassinated and hundreds disappeared by the security forces 'on mere suspicion that some among them supported the Shining Path.'[63] Both international humanitarian law and human rights law prohibit such arbitrary and punitive measures.

Juvenile delinquency and discipline problems. Delinquency has reportedly increased in El Salvador since the armed cease-fire in early 1992. Some argue that there is just increased media coverage, while others insist that armed robberies on the highways increased as soldiers and members of the security forces realized they were soon to be discharged. In late 1992, UNICEF's Mozambique office worried that RENAMO would be unable to control the estimated 8,000 boy soldiers who would be roaming the countryside, armed and unfed. Recent reports from Mozambique allege that RENAMO has a tighter control over its troops than previously supposed, but so far no one knows whether either the government or the RENAMO troops will respond to the order to disarm.[64] Juvenile delinquency among Liberian ex-combatants is also predicted by local and international relief workers.

---

61   *Id.* at 17-18.

62   See for example, 'House Demolitions', *Information Sheet: Update*, B'Tselem, Jerusalem, 1 Jun. 1989, p.5; 'House Demolition and Sealing as a Form of Punishment in the West Bank and Gaza Strip', *Information Sheet: Update November 1990*, B'Tselem, Jerusalem.

63   *Peru: Civil Society and Democracy under Fire*, Americas Watch, vol.IV, no.6, August 1992, p.13.

64   Bill Keller, 'Mozambique's Outlook Brightens as Truce Holds and Drought Ends,' *New York Times*, 22 Feb. 1993, A1, A6.

Numerous reports cite discipline problems among young former combatants and participants in civil strife. A teacher working with a Palestinian human rights organization links the prevalence of such problems in schools and families to the frustration youth feel at having had the trappings of power, but no real control over their situation. She feels that parents, overwhelmed with the daily problems of just living, deal with their children in an authoritarian manner. At the same time, the *intifada* has disrupted traditional family structures so that the authority of fathers and grandfathers carries less weight with children, themselves thrust suddenly into authoritative roles.

It is not clear whether the level of discipline imposed on child soldiers in combat influences post-war discipline problems. Uganda's NRA children reportedly obeyed a code of conduct, were reliable, trustworthy and did not abuse the civilian population, but we have found no follow-up data on post-war delinquency among them. Boy soldiers with Liberia's INPFL faction allegedly complied with Prince Johnson's 'do as I say or die' brand of discipline. Liberian NGO staff anticipate that they may in turn defy routine disciplinary measures, much as Charles Taylor's boys, used to the respect commanded by a gun, are unlikely to submit to the discipline of a parent or a teacher. In Northern Ireland, youth who have grown up with violence are said to have lost all notion of fear as well as any concept of peace, and consequently are difficult to discipline.[65]

Caring for the homeless or orphaned. In Uganda the numbers of war-orphaned children and ex-child soldiers were extremely high. We have no recent information on how the government or society dealt with the burden of housing and caring for them. Mozambique, Somalia, and Liberia, among others, are likely to face a similar situation. While orphaned or homeless child victims are surely more numerous than similarly situated child soldiers, the latter group may be more difficult to accommodate given all of their experiences and the many consequences, described above.

---

65   L. McNeil, 'The Kids are not Alright,' *Spin*, Jan. 1989, p.24.

5

Responding to the
Consequences of Participation:
Law, Programmes and Policy

AP Photo
Germany, 1945. 14-year old prisoners of war.

Fernando Moleres – IMPACT VISUALS
Los Ranchos, Chalate, El Salvador, May 1992. Young FMLN members at school.

Patrick Robert – SYGMA
Congotown near Monrovia, Liberia, 9 August 1990. Machine gun and school bag.

THE GENERAL THRUST behind national and international action on behalf of children is the recognition of their need for special care and protection, including legal protection.

5.1 The Child as Protected Person

In the words of the Preamble to the 1989 Convention on the Rights of the Child (CRC), 'the child should be fully prepared to live an individual life in society, and brought up in the spirit of the ideals proclaimed in the Charter of the United Nations...' Other international instruments stress the developmental needs of the child—freedom from hunger, access to education, participation in social and cultural life—and the particular role of the family. The CRC uniquely embraces the whole spectrum of children's rights, specifically endorsing the basic principle of the best interests of the child in a total regime oriented to his or her development and self-fulfilment.

5.1.1 The Child entitled to 'General Protection'

The Fourth Geneva Convention, 'relative to the protection of civilian persons in time of war', contains numerous provisions benefiting or protecting children, both as civilians and in their own right.[1] *Common Article 3* extends a measure of minimum protection to persons taking no active part in non-international armed conflicts. Child soldiers who have laid down their arms and those placed *hors de combat* by sickness, wounds, detention, or any other cause are entitled to the protection due to all such non-participants,[2] and in particular to the benefit of rules regulating the conduct of hostilities. These include the basic distinction between civilians and combatants, and the principle prohibiting attacks on civilian targets.[3]

---

1   A civilian includes anyone who is not a member of the armed forces or of an organized armed group of a party to the conflict. Civilians may not be subject to deliberate personal attack, since they pose no immediate threat to the adversary. See Bothe, M., Partsch, K. & Solf, W., *New Rules for Victims of Armed Conflicts*, 1982, 292-6. Curiously, during the inter-war period, efforts to promote the protection of civilians were seen by some as 'a disservice to the cause of peace ...[T]he assumption that the effects of war might extend to non-belligerents hardly seemed compatible with the efforts then being made to restrict the very concept of belligerent.' See ICRC, *The Work of the ICRC for the Benefit of Civilian Detainees in German Concentration Camps between 1939 and 1945*, (1975).

2   Relevant to detained child soldiers, *Common Article 3* prohibits violence to life and person, outrages upon personal dignity, and the passing of sentences and the carrying out of executions without previous judgment pronounced by a regularly constituted court, affording all the judicial guarantees which are recognized as indispensable by civilized peoples. For text, see above Chapter 2.

3   API art. 51(1)(2); APII art. 13, provides similarly.

5.1.2 The Child entitled to 'Special Protection'

In recognition of their particular needs and vulnerability, children benefit from specific provisions of the Fourth Geneva Convention, so-called *special protection*, such as that obliging States to allow the free passage of assistance intended for children under 15 and expectant mothers (GC4, art. 23); or requiring the occupying power to facilitate the good functioning of institutions for the care of children in occupied territory (GC4, art. 50(1)); or obliging a party to conflict to provide support to the dependants of internees or food supplements to interned children (GC4, art. 81(3)).[4]

The 1977 Additional Protocols go further, expressly confirming the special protection due to children. Article 77 of *Additional Protocol I*, entitled 'Protection of Children', declares in its opening paragraph that

> Children shall be the object of special respect and shall be protected against any form of indecent assault. The Parties to the conflict shall provide them with the care and aid they require, whether because of their age or for any other reason.

Article 4 of *Additional Protocol II* confirms the obligation to provide children with the requisite care and aid, referring expressly to education, family reunion, limitations on recruitment, and temporary evacuation.

Both the Geneva Conventions and the Additional Protocols repeatedly link the protection of the child to the maintenance of *family life*.[5] In cases of internment, families should be kept together wherever possible (GC4, art. 82; API, art. 77(4)), for example, and every effort must be made to promote the reunion of families separated by reason of armed conflict (API, art. 74; APII, art. 4(3)(b)). The general intent, so far as possible, is to preserve family life and, by inference, the natural process of child development. Similar objectives are clear in the human rights context, where States have recognized that the family should receive 'protection by society and the State'; and that 'special measures of protection and assistance should be taken on behalf of all children and young persons.'[6]

These policy objectives cannot be overemphasized. Duly strengthened by international recognition of the principle of the best interests of the child

---

4   A complete account of the provisions intended to benefit children during armed conflict is beyond the scope of the present analysis. Some twenty-five articles in the Geneva Conventions and the Additional Protocols deal with the special protection of children.

5   This dimension is fully examined in Singer, S., 'The protection of children during armed conflict situations,' *International Review of the Red Cross*, May-June 1986, 133.

6   Art. 23(1), 1966 Covenant on Civil and Political Rights; and Art. 10(3), 1966 Covenant on Economic, Social and Cultural Rights, respectively.

as a primary consideration in the CRC,[7] they highlight the exceptional nature of 'officially' removing the child from the family environment by way of conscription or enrolment.

5.1.3 The Responsibility to Ensure Protection

In an ideal world, the child's best interest lies in never having to join an armed group and in never having to live under conditions which make that the only choice in the other battle for survival. Not living in an ideal world, our recommendations concerning the protection of child soldiers often have to deal with consequences, not just prevention. And in seeking to ensure that the consequences suffered by children who participate in war are addressed, the sources of obligation must be clarified, and those to whom the responsibility attaches must be identified. Unfortunately the provisions of international humanitarian law are not always as clear as they might be.

Under Common Article 1 of the four Geneva Conventions and article 1.1 of Additional Protocol I, the High Contracting Parties, that is the ratifying States, undertake to respect and to ensure respect for those treaties in all circumstances. The Geneva Conventions generally place the responsibility to ensure protection in international conflicts on the State party having jurisdiction and control over certain groups or individuals, for example, prisoners of war or an occupied civilian population. Except for limited provisions protecting the entire population of a country in conflict, the Geneva Conventions do not regulate the relationship between nationals of a country and their own government. The Fourth Geneva Convention requires an occupying power to respect the physical integrity, family rights or religious rights of 'protected persons'; moreover, an occupying power must address the educational needs of the children of the occupied population, even though the Geneva Conventions impose no similar obligations with respect to its own nationals.

Additional Protocol I offers an opportunity for NGEs involved in an 'internationalized' conflict within the terms of article 1(4), unilaterally to declare their adherence to the Geneva Conventions and the Additional Protocol; for that reason many of the latter's provisions, such as article 77 on recruitment, bind 'all parties to the conflict', as opposed only to States. Additional Protocol I also increases the protection afforded the civilian population and obliges parties to the conflict to respect the fundamental rights of all persons under their jurisdiction or control, and several articles mention humane treatment, due process for detainees and 'special protection' for children. Additional Protocol I does not *explicitly* oblige

---

7   Art. 3(1), 1989 Convention on the Rights of the Child.

parties to the conflict to ensure other basic rights, such as education, physical or mental health, freedom of religion, association or expression, but much of this is covered by the totality of international humanitarian law, including the four Geneva Conventions, which enter through operation of the Protocol.

Additional Protocol II contains no article calling on States to respect and ensure respect for its provisions, although the provision in *Common Article 3* is equally applicable to non-international armed conflicts. Additional Protocol II also offers no explicit opportunity for armed opposition groups formally to declare their adherence to the Protocol; opposition groups can simply give notice of their intention to abide by the Protocol, as did the FMLN in El Salvador and the NPA in the Philippines, but such a decarlation is anyway unnecessary where the objective conditions of article 1 are satisfied. *Common Article 3*, also applicable in internal armed conflicts, refers to each party to the conflict, so that these minimum customary international law standards extend beyond the category of ratifying States. That being said, however, both legal and practical difficulties follow, not the least being the absence of enforcement or monitoring machinery.

Given the limited reach of the Additional Protocols, the Convention on the Rights of the Child and other international human rights instruments are extremely important in ensuring that States parties respect the rights and respond to the needs of current and former child soldiers under their jurisdiction. Unlike many other human rights treaties, the CRC has no general derogation clause allowing States to suspend certain rights in time of emergency. Consequently, in certain cases the CRC ensures that children are even better protected than adults.[8] Moreover, States parties to the CRC undertake to 'respect and ensure the rights' proclaimed to 'each child within their jurisdiction'. This means, for example, that a former child soldier who takes refuge in the territory of a State party to the CRC benefits as much from its provisions as do child nationals of that country. In short, responsibility to protect or respond to the needs of child soldiers may fall on States or NGEs, as parties or adherents to international instruments, as parties to the conflict, as subjects of national law, or by reason of customary international law. However, it is often the case that fulfilment of the formal requirements is complicated by lack of political will and the practical resource limitations that occur in any conflict. Certain obligations, of

---

8 See Cohn, I., 'The Convention on the Rights of the Child: What it Means for Children in War,' 3 *Int'l J. Refugee Law* 291 (1991); under the CRC, there is thus no possibility to derogate from arts. 37, 40 (torture, arbitrary detention, administration of justice guarantees).

course, such as those relating to physical integrity, humane treatment, and freedom from torture, are never dependent on the availability of resources, but must be fulfilled by all parties concerned.

5.1.4 The Practicalities of Providing Protection: When and Where to Intervene

Even when legal responsibilities are undertaken and acknowledged by States or by armed groups, the circumstances of war can make implementation of certain children's rights difficult or impossible. For example, if the children of a brutalized population seek to join an armed group which refuses to admit those under fifteen as required by international law, who can realistically be expected to care for them? Had the Ugandan NRA turned away the hundreds of orphans whose families had been killed by government troops, it could scarcely have been required or expected to build nurseries or employ staff to care for and educate the children. In El Salvador, it is doubtful if it would have been in the best interests of children to be sent out of FMLN-controlled zones, away from the adults closest to them who may have been involved in the struggle. Where opposition forces retain territory and enjoy relative stability, positive steps to meet certain needs of children and youth may be feasible.

States will encounter practical difficulties in fulfilling responsibilities towards child soldiers and children affected by war. The Salvadoran government had no access to provide education in FMLN-controlled zones, and in all likelihood the remaining populations preferred to develop their own social infrastructure. A population or group that blames its government for abuses or rights violations is unlikely to request or accept responsive efforts that do not address the original violation. Arguably, Israel is obliged under article 39 of the CRC to provide psychological services for Palestinian children abused or traumatized by their detention for participation in the *intifada*. Many Palestinian psychologists we spoke with, however, would insist that Israeli security forces respect the rights of detainees, and reject the argument for mental health services on the grounds that therapy provided by Israel would aim to help children adjust to the occupation.

Local and international NGOs thus have a major responsibility to address the needs of populations and child soldiers in zones under NGE control; and NGEs in turn should not unnecessarily hinder access to the population.

5.2   Responding to Detention Issues

5.2.1 Detention in International Human Rights Law

The Covenant on Civil and Political Rights ensures the right to liberty and security of the person, to freedom from arbitrary arrest and detention, and stipulates that all persons deprived of their liberty are to be treated with humanity and respect and all shall be equal before the courts.[9] Article 10 of the Covenant provides that 'Accused juvenile persons shall be separated from adults', and that 'Juvenile offenders shall be segregated from adults and be accorded treatment appropriate to their age and legal status.' However, the Covenant, like most human rights treaties, permits States to take measures derogating from the due process rights of the detained and the accused, 'in time of public emergency which threatens the life of the nation.'[10]

The Convention on the Rights of the Child, however, contains no general derogation clause and the rights of detained and accused children may not be limited even in time of public emergency or war. Article 37 stresses that,

> (b) ... The arrest, detention or imprisonment of a child shall be used *only as a measure of last resort and for the shortest appropriate period of time*;
> (c) Every child deprived of liberty shall be treated with humanity and respect for the inherent dignity of the human person, and in a manner which takes into account the needs of persons of their age. In particular, every child deprived of liberty shall be separated from adults unless it is considered in the child's best interest not to do so and shall have the right to maintain contact with his/her family through correspondence and visits, save in exceptional circumstances. (Emphasis supplied)

Article 40(3) follows United Nations standard-setting efforts by recognizing the need for juvenile justice procedures specifically for children alleged to have violated the criminal law, as well as the desirability

---

9   See Arts. 9, 10, 14, 26.

10   Article 4(1). Human rights treaties generally stipulate certain fundamental rights as never subject to derogation. Article 4(2) of the Covenant permits no derogation from those provisions which guarantee the right to life, the right to recognition as a person before the law and the right to freedom of conscience, thought and religion, or which forbid torture or inhuman treatment, slavery, servitude, or conviction or punishment under retroactive laws. See also, European Convention, arts. 2, 3, 4(1) and 7; 1969 American Convention, art. 27.

of establishing a minimum age of criminal responsibility, with due emphasis on alternatives to institutional care.[11]

5.2.2 Detention in International Humanitarian Law applicable in International Armed Conflicts

Young persons between 15 and 18 years of age who, in an international armed conflict, are enroled or take part in a mass uprising of the civilian population benefit from combatant status, and therefore enjoy prisoner of war status automatically if captured.[12] A child under fifteen who, contrary to international humanitarian law, was recruited or enroled in the armed forces, should also benefit: 'there is ... no age limit for entitlement to prisoner of war status; age may simply be a factor justifying privileged treatment.'[13] The nature of the obligation is to condemn the conduct of the parties to the conflict, with whom lies responsibility for the breach, not to penalize the participants.

Article 77(4) of Additional Protocol I provides that, 'If arrested, detained or interned for reasons related to the armed conflict, children shall be held in quarters separate from the quarters of adults, except where families are accommodated as family units as provided in Article 75, paragraph 5.' No age limit is set: 'Whether persons of 16, 17 or 18 years of age would have to be detained separately from adults is left to national law, tradition and the decision of the parties to the conflict.'[14] Article 11 of Additional Protocol I, oriented to medical well-being, provides that the physical or mental health and integrity of persons 'interned, detained or otherwise deprived of liberty' for reasons related to armed conflict shall not be endangered by any unjustified act or omission, and that any such wilful act or omission shall be a grave breach of the Protocol.[15]

---

11 The United Nations has taken several steps to promote minimum standards of treatment on behalf of those whose situation might otherwise expose them to abuse. Relevant principles, at the 'soft law' level, include the UN Standard Minimum Rules for the Treatment of Prisoners, the Standard Minimum Rules for the Administration of Juvenile Justice, the Code of Conduct of Law Enforcement Officials and the Principles of Medical Ethics relevant to the Role of Health Personnel, particularly Physicians, in the Protection of Prisoners and Detainees against Torture and other Cruel, Inhuman or Degrading Treatment or Punishment.

12 See API, art. 43(2); on entitlement to prisoner of war status, see GC3, art. 4A.

13 Dutli, María Teresa, 'Captured Child Combatants,' *International Review of the Red Cross,* Sept.-Oct. 1990, 421-34. A child who takes part in hostilities but is not a combatant within the meaning of international humanitarian law, is subject to local legislation, but also takes the benefits of articles 45, 75 and 77.

14 Bothe, Partsch and Solf, *New Rules,* 478.

15 See generally, Bothe, Partsch and Solf, *New Rules,* 109-16.

5.2.3 Detention in International Humanitarian Law applicable in Non-international Armed Conflict

In a non-international armed conflict, a detained child participant remains subject to the local law; there is no prisoner of war status, and no category of protected persons or civilian internee from which to benefit. The *application* of the local law is subject to age considerations, however, and in appropriate cases to the overriding provisions of *Common Article 3* and article 4 of Additional Protocol II. Together these articles ensure humane treatment and respect for the person, honour, convictions and religious practices of, among others, detained child participants or detained children suspected of participation in hostilities. Article 4(3) includes detailed provisions for the education and family reunion of *all* children, including those under fifteen who have participated in hostilities and been captured. Moreover, the death penalty may be neither pronounced nor executed on a person under eighteen at the time of the offence in question.

Article 5 of Additional Protocol II deals specifically with the conditions of detention of persons deprived of their liberty for reasons related to the armed conflict, 'whether they are interned or detained'.[16] Paragraph (1) refers to the health, nutrition, hygiene, religious freedom and labour conditions to which detainees are entitled. Paragraph (2) obliges those responsible for the internment or detention, 'within the limits of their capabilities', to respect additional provisions, for example, on the separate accommodation of women and men, unless in the case of a family accommodated together; sending and receiving letters; location away from combat zones; medical examination; and protection of physical and mental integrity.

Going beyond *Common Article 3*, which makes no special provision for the protection of persons detained for reasons related to a non-international armed conflict, article 5 'introduces new elements into international humanitarian law,'[17] moving the standard of protection nearer to that applying to prisoners of war. It applies both to military and civilians, the participant as well as the supporter interned for that reason.[18] Despite the minimum rules laid down in article 5, no special status accrues to those detained, and local law continues to apply, for example, with respect to the responsibility for acts. Due process guarantees, with their basis in international human rights law, are expressly guaranteed by Article 6.

16   See also art. 2(2): 'At the end of the armed conflict, all the persons who have been deprived of their liberty or whose liberty has been restricted for reasons related to such conflict, as well as those deprived of their liberty or whose liberty is restricted after the conflict for the same reasons, shall enjoy the protection of Articles 5 and 6 until the end of such deprivation or restriction of liberty.'

17   Bothe, Partsch and Solf, *New Rules*, p. 645.

18   Ibid.

5.2.4 Programme and Policy Interventions

The Mandate and Role of the ICRC. The ICRC's role with respect to prisoners of war and detainees is long-standing. The Geneva Conventions contain express legal entitlement, described by Hans-Peter Gasser as, 'an absolute right of access, except when precluded by imperative military necessity. An authority which improperly forbids delegates access to [all places of detention, indeed all places where there are protected persons] would directly violate its obligations under the Conventions.'[19] In addition, the Xth International Red Cross Conference held in Geneva in 1921, expressed the view that 'political detainees in time of civil war' should be treated by analogy with prisoners of war.[20]

In practice, the agreement of the interested party, either government or opposition, is indispensable to effective action. With respect to internal conflicts, Common Article 3 notes that 'An impartial humanitarian body, such as the International Committee of the Red Cross, may offer its services to the Parties to the conflict.' In practice, this can be hard to negotiate, and involvement by the ICRC is not helped by the uncompromising endorsement of the principle of non-intervention 'for any reason whatever', in article 3 of Additional Protocol II.[21]

Gaining access is difficult in many situations, as is ensuring access in accordance with ICRC criteria.[22] Delegates can never be absolutely certain

---

19 H.P. Gasser, 'Scrutiny,' 9 *Aust. YB Int'l Law* 345, 355 (1985).

20 Xth International Red Cross Conference, Geneva, 1921, Resolution No. 6. See also XVIth International Red Cross Conference, London, 1938, Resolution No. XIV: humane treatment for all political prisoners, respect of the life and liberty of non-combatants, effective measures for the protection of children; XXth International Red Cross Conference, Vienna, 1965, Resolution No. XXXI: considering that sufficient protection for the victims of non-international conflicts and internal disturbances, in particular the prisoners and detainees, has not been sufficient, recognizing the applicability of the provisions of common article 3, and urging the ICRC to continue its work with the aim of strengthening the humanitarian assistance of the Red Cross to the victims of non-international conflicts.

21 Art. 3 provides: '1. Nothing in this Protocol shall be invoked for the purpose of affecting the sovereignty of a State or the responsibility of the government, by all legitimate means, to maintain or re-establish law and order in the State or to defend the national unity and territorial integrity of the State. 2. Nothing in this Protocol shall be invoked as a justification for intervening, directly or indirectly, for any reason whatever, in the armed conflict or in the internal or external affairs of the High Contracting Party in the territory of which that conflict occurs.'

22 The ICRC's conditions are: visits without witnesses, repeated visits, visits to all detainees of the category covered by the agreement with the government in question; see Jäckli R., 'What does the Future hold for International Humanitarian Law?' 9 *Aust. Y.B.Int'l. Law* 384, 388 (1985).

they are seeing all the detainees.[23] A Salvadoran FMLN ex-combatant, who was detained at the age of 16 on suspicion of participation in terrorist activities, claimed he was hidden in a bathroom when ICRC delegates came to interview detainees. He later received the soap and other items left by the delegates, but was not permitted to meet them. In Sri Lanka, the ICRC's access is predicated on the government's acceptance of an 'offre de service'. In the five years from 1987-1992, ICRC delegates were able to visit some 47 JVP (Sinhalese) detainees under the age of 18 and approximately 44 persons (Tamils) under age 18 detained as a result of the conflict in the north and east (the vast majority of whom are not known to have been young combatants).[24] The ICRC is denied access to Tamils detained by the LTTE in the north, and cannot be certain of having complete access to all those detained by the government security forces. In addition to possible limitations on access, the ICRC's detention visits are restricted in scope to an examination of the physical conditions of the detention and the detainees. In certain cases, delegates may be able to monitor judicial guarantees.

Hans-Peter Gasser has also emphasized that the ICRC is not a judicial body, and that to conduct an inquiry under the Geneva Conventions, for example, would compromise its neutrality. Confronted with breaches of international humanitarian law, however, ICRC delegates may react, and intervene to stop the violation and to prevent its repetition; such intervention is generally confidential and secondary to action to aid the victim.[25] In cases of detained minors, delegates might refer to the relevant Geneva Conventions and Protocols, for example, to advocate for the separation of children from adults (API, art. 77(4)). Even this is not always easily implemented, either because children and adults prefer to remain together, as is the case, for example, with detained Palestinians in the Israeli occupied territories, or because separate facilities are not available.

While the ICRC's crucial detention visits cannot be jeopardized by an expansion of their practice to include inspection of due process for the detained, human rights organizations, local NGOs, and United Nations agencies have an important, complementary role to play.

The Role of Local NGOs. NGOs operating in the highly politicized context of war or strife often have difficult access to detainees or to the legal system, and few NGOs can afford to devote limited resources to the needs or rights of detained children and youth. Yet efforts to keep track of persons detained or suspected of having been detained, to establish hotlines

---

23   As noted above, the ICRC had no access to Ethiopian soldiers detained by the EPLF, and the ICRC has not always had regular access to all persons detained in Peru.

24   Information provided to Ilene Cohn during visit to Sri Lanka in Nov. 1992.

25   H.-P. Gasser, above note 19, pp. 355-6.

facilitating communication of information to families of the detained, to provide legal advice and counsel to the detained, to expose unsatisfactory detention conditions, and to document injustices in the detention or penal process, occasionally prove productive. If these efforts do not produce the desired outcome in each individual case, they nonetheless keep the issues on the public agenda and undoubtedly offer hope to the detained. The psychosocial and physical consequences of the capture, detention, interrogation or incarceration of children accused or convicted of participation in armed conflict should also be a focus of NGO efforts.

5.3   Addressing the Psychosocial Consequences

5.3.1 The Legal Framework for Action

Dealing with the psychosocial consequences of children's involvement in conflict mostly and necessarily takes part at national and community level. However, international legal obligations do offer a set of general principles and a framework for action. Article 77 of Additional Protocol I requires the Parties to the conflict to provide children 'with the care and aid they require, whether because of their age or any other reason.'[26] The reference to 'age or any other reason' can be interpreted to include the trauma resulting from involvement in combat, and as therefore implying an obligation to provide appropriate counselling or other rehabilitation services. Such a view is supported by article 39 of the Convention on the Rights of the Child:

> States Parties shall take all appropriate measures to promote the physical
> and psychological recovery and social re-integration of a child victim of:
> any form of neglect, exploitation, or abuse; torture or any other form of
> cruel, inhuman or degrading treatment or punishment; or armed conflicts.
> Such recovery and re-integration shall take place in an environment which
> fosters the health, self-respect and dignity of the child.

Other international provisions stress the centrality of the family and its entitlement to protection, or emphasize the principle of family unity. Both are 'organizing principles' that can contribute substantially to responses to the psychosocial consequences of participation in war.

In practice, however, conflict is often synonymous with the breakdown of community programmes and support systems, with limited access to those in need of services, and frequent suspicion of those seeking to provide

26   API, art. 77(1).

assistance where parties are polarized by politics or race. In such circumstances, political and legal avenues for redress at regional and international level may be useful, if only to publicise needs and mobilize world opinion.

5.3.2 The Need for Further Research

Effective interventions to address the psychosocial impact of war on children should be grounded on a local assessment of options and possibilities, identification of those most likely to suffer crippling consequences or to benefit from constructive outcomes, and the development of culturally appropriate means of preventing or minimizing the former and bolstering the latter. Such research is not always thought feasible or worthwhile, but in practice it has yielded informative data and innovative, responsive programmes. Most existing research, however, addresses the psychosocial impact of war on children without necessarily focusing on the child soldier or participant in hostilities.[27] The number of active child participants is always less than that of children victims of war; many participants and victims will have faced the same traumatic experiences, but some portion of research and programme resources should be devoted to the former group of youngsters and to the even larger number of adults who spent their entire childhoods as active combatants.

The development and dissemination of sound assessment tools that can be adapted easily to local circumstances and used to get a picture of where the most acute psychosocial needs lie, would be constructive. International agencies and NGOs could train local child-care specialists to adapt measures, collect and analyze data and use their results in programme development. A training-of-trainers approach, both to research and programme development, has been the method of choice among NGOs in Mozambique, El Salvador, Liberia and elsewhere.

---

27   In a study of Lebanese children's war-related experiences and psychosocial outcomes, only 2.7% of the 224 children between 10-16 years old in the sample reported having actively participated in the civil war; see Mona Macksoud and J. Lawrence Aber, 'The War Experiences and Psychosocial Development of Children in Lebanon,' *Child Development*, (in press) 1993. In a similar study conducted in El Salvador, only 4.5% of the sample reported active participation in hostilities; see José Luis Henriquez y Milagros Mendez, 'Los Efectos Psicosociales de la Guerra en Niños de El Salvador', *Revista de Psicologia de El Salvador*, vol.XI, no.44, (1992), 89-107, UCA, San Salvador. A study of Kuwaiti children after the Gulf War found that 41.3% of the 11-16 year olds interviewed had participated in the Kuwaiti resistance, for example, by carrying arms, patrolling neighbourhoods, distributing pamphlets or food, changing addresses to confuse the Iraqis. However, the psychosocial symptoms of this group on its own were not analyzed; see Mona Macksoud, Fatima Nazar, 'The Impact of the Iraqi Occupation on the Psychosocial Development of Children in Kuwait', The Kuwaiti Society for the Advancement of Arab Children, 1 Mar. 1993.

A study of the factors on which to base predictions of successful reconciliation, such as culture, resolution of the root causes of the conflict, popular perceptions of the conflict resolution process, and the material outcome of the conflict, might help international politicians and local groups structure a durable peace. With regard to the re-integration of ex-combatants, it would be helpful to have studies of identity formation among child combatants and young adults who spent their youth as combatants, and the problems they face in reconciling to a civilian identity.

We have seen no programmes for ex-child soldiers that have been seriously evaluated, and no cross-country comparisons of problems or programmes. Researchers need to investigate the effectiveness of existing programme models, and whether they might be replicated in other contexts.

5.3.3 Development and Implementation of Responsive Programmes

Whether a responsive programme is implemented in war-time or during the transition to peace, for victims, ex-combatants or both, experts from different regions of the world have suggested several guidelines to successful programme development and execution.

Existing support structures, including mothers or other significant adult caregivers such as grandparents and teachers, must be reinforced. As a preventive measure, efforts to shield children from the most harmful psychosocial consequences of conflict, such as assisting mothers, families and communities to support their children and maintain a reassuring environment, might help to dissuade some children from leaving to join an armed group.

The Gaza Community Mental Health Programme, for example, trains parents to help prepare children for the next traumatic experience and trains mothers and teachers to recognize and respond to psychosocial symptoms at home and in school. A 'School for Health Promoters' and a 'School for Parents', developed at the Central American University (UCA) in El Salvador, train community health promoters and parents from scores of communities in ex-conflict zones to recognize mental health symptoms in children and to build easily-implemented responses into their daily routines. The trainees in these programmes have themselves lived through numerous, severely traumatic experiences. The director of the School for Promoters observed that many health promoters responded personally to the training sessions, taking the opportunity to recognize and address some of their own psychosocial reactions to their past. Caretakers' and programme staff's mental health needs must be acknowledged and addressed, before they can be expected to be of optimal benefit to traumatized children.

The development of intervention strategies should consider incorporating traditional practices, values and beliefs. Filipino psychologists maintain that recognition and incorporation of traditional values, aspects of local belief systems or religious rituals, speeds the healing process in adults and children. Psychologists working with former child soldiers in Mozambique have made similar assertions and have developed their interventions accordingly.

From 1987-1989 the Sri Lankan government's counter-insurgency campaign against JVP rebels claimed about 20,000 lives, with some estimates going as high as 60,000. Many of those reported missing or killed in the south were youth under 18 years of age and several thousand young persons were detained. By now most have been released or, after three to five years of detention, are presumed to be adults. The government perceived moral deterioration among youth as a precursor to the uprising and developed a rehabilitation programme based on Buddhist philosophy, involving an investigation of the youths' past problems, from one to three months training at a temple where 'the youth is provided all possible facilities to mould his character and vision according to the Buddhist Philosophy', and two to three weeks of meditation, culminating in vocational training and conditional release.[28]

Deinstitutionalization of treatment implies community-based strategies that reduce the stigma attached to psychological therapy while taking advantage of existing human and material resources. The focus is on the 'illness' in the relationship between society and the individual, as opposed to the individual alone.[29] Some Salvadoran psychologists insist that traditional concepts of mental health (acceptance of and adaptation to social norms and values) and mental illness (deviation from this norm) have lost all legitimacy in contexts where the abnormal (war, violence, loss, mistrust, latent fear), has become the norm. In such a situation, traditional forms of mental health treatment (individual doctor-patient therapy) risk being perceived by the majority as attempts to promote adaptation to the status quo—a danger also foreseen by Palestinian psychologists.

Filipino psychologists have used a holistic, integrated approach to helping which 'takes into account the whole person or child in the context of the family, community and society.'[30] In the midst of Liberia's civil war

28   *A Brief on Rehabilitation of Youth in Sri Lanka*, Secretariat of the Commissioner General of Rehabilitation, Ministry of Youth Affairs & Sports (undated).

29   Ernesto Attias and Ilene Cohn, *Infancia y Guerra: Informe sobre El Impacto Psicosocial de la Violencia en los Niños de America Central*, UNICEF Area Office for Central America, Mar. 1990.

30   Elizabeth Marcelino, 'Children at War', *Children of the Storm*, vol.3, no.1, Children's Rehabilitation Center, Manila, July 1991-March 1992, p.29.

a local NGO produced a short, straight-forward brochure for parents and caretakers, listing groups of children at risk, including child soldiers, behaviour that may indicate a need for help, and 'suggestions of what to do', employable in any environment.[31]

Deinstitutionalization also suggests that former combatants be treated as members of a larger community. Offering special treatment such as loans or scholarships risks stigmatizing ex-combatants or engendering resentment among community-members who have often been war-victims themselves. Accordingly, Neil Boothby stressed the reunification of former RENAMO child soldiers with their families and gradually closed down the centre in the Mozambican capital where they had temporarily been housed. In the interim, he devised a treatment strategy drawing on traditional activities, such as story-telling, dance, theatre, socio-drama and art. A training-of-trainers programme enabled 500 Mozambican provincial and district workers to assist communities to respond to the psychosocial needs of war-affected children, both victims and victimizers.[32]

Complementing the principle of deinstitutionalization and community-based interventions, is the *practice and desirability of adapting existing programmes to include former combatants*. UNICEF's psychosocial project in the Israeli occupied territories aims to develop and promote local models for psychological health care for traumatized children, but does not distinguish between participants and victims.[33] UNICEF hopes to upgrade staff at existing mental health centres, train teachers and health workers in schools and at summer camps to recognize at-risk youth, and provide support to parents, in particular mothers, in dealing with traumatized children.[34]

Several local and international organizations based in Liberia forecast huge numbers of traumatized child soldiers. The Liberian Opportunities Industrialization Center (LOIC) and UNICEF are preparing assessment techniques and projects for training health and education personnel in war trauma counselling. Existing UNICEF and local NGO programmes for disadvantaged youth already include a number of former child combatants. LOIC, which traditionally has run vocational counselling programmes, lost a number of students to armed groups and is now planning for their

31   Marion Subah and Delores Friesen, *Trauma Healing for Children*, Brochure produced for the Christian Health Association of Liberia, Monrovia (1992).

32   Neil Boothby, 'Working in the War Zone: A Look at Psychological Theory and Practice from the Field', *Mind & Human Interaction*, vol.2, no.2, Virginia, 1990, p.35.

33   *The Strategy for the 1992-1994 UNICEF Programme of Cooperation in the West Bank and Gaza Strip*, UNICEF West Bank and Gaza Strip, Jun. 1992, p.10.

34   *The Situation of Palestinian Children in the West Bank and Gaza Strip* (Draft), UNICEF West Bank and Gaza Strip, Jerusalem, Jul. 1992, p.96.

reincorporation. Obstacles to success in Liberia include the continuing conflict and the serious lack of professional human resources.[35]

The Liberian National Reconciliation Commission (NRC) is an example of how difficult it is to mount an entirely new institution aimed at the rehabilitation and reintegration of former combatants. In a country completely devastated by on-going civil war, where entire communities have been displaced, killed, left without shelter or means of self-support, the NRC aimed to 'assist in altering the attitudes and values of former combatants, transform their lives, integrate them in society, resettle them in various communities and re-unite them with their families and relatives.'[36] Unfortunately, on the occasion of our visit in November 1992, the major goals were still distant dreams. Family tracing and reunification were frustrated by restricted access to most of the country, and vocational training made little sense in the absence of a job market. Most of the 14-23 rehabilitation sites chosen for the project were located in Taylor-held territory and the NRC lacked sufficient funds even to run the Monrovia-based centre. Over slightly more than a year the NRC had put six groups of ex-combatants, totalling some 381 persons, through 'Phase 1' (guidance, psychological and vocational training); an estimated 10-20% were between 9-19 years old. Very few had found jobs or become self-sufficient, and their families were mostly off-limits in Taylor territory and unable to support them. The NRC's fifth quarterly evaluation for July-September 1992 reported that graduates had stormed the offices complaining of lack of food, lodging, medication, school fees, clothing and shoes—the very things that had enticed them to join the programme in the first place. By November 1992, the NRC's director was advocating a revised approach: rebuild the rural infrastructure, return all former combatants to their home communities, if they still exist, and provide education and services via the national infrastructure.

Forgiveness and reconciliation. Neil Boothby suggests that '[t]he former child soldier needs to be forgiven by society, sometimes by the very people who have been victimized by his actions.'[37] In Mozambique, that conviction has been translated into efforts to help community members, police, teachers, and soldiers, to understand that these boys were also

---

35   Reginald K. Hodges, 'Victims of Traumatic Experiences and the Healing Process: A View of Psychological Problems Resulting from the Liberia Civil Conflict', Opportunities Industrialization Centres International, PA (no date)—an account by LOIC's Director of Program Development of his impressions of the psychological effects of the conflict on youth and former combatants, though without distinguishing between children and adults.

36   'Facts about the National Re-adjustment Commission', brochure produced by the National Re-adjustment Commission, Monrovia.

37   N. Boothby, 'Living in the War Zone,' *World Refugee Survey - 1989 in Review*, p. 41.

victims; and into national level policy initiatives to ensure amnesty, family reunification and follow-up social support. But in Liberia, very few turned in their guns when the interim government declared an amnesty; those who did were mainly near enough to the capital to have heard of training and support programmes or other incentives to disarm. The remainder either did not know, or felt that without jobs, homes, and communities to return to, the gun continued to offer greater security. The successful disarming of combatants clearly needs more than just an amnesty. Indeed, an amnesty in the name of national reconciliation or psychosocial healing can have negative consequences. Latin American psychologists from countries such as Chile, Argentina, and Uruguay, where amnesties have sanctioned impunity for known perpetrators of serious human rights violations, note high levels of latent fear, mistrust, and self-censoring behaviour among civil society, even in peace-time. People lack confidence in the capability of the machinery of social justice, including the police and the judiciary, to prevent or respond to violations of the rule of law. In El Salvador, FMLN political leaders voted against the government sponsored general amnesty passed in March 1993.

Depending on the context, an amnesty may speed the psychosocial recovery of some victimizers but may also put the fragile mental health of victims at continued risk. Public acknowledgement of and accountability for human rights violations are important steps towards national reconciliation. Abuses of the rights of children in armed conflict should be strictly monitored and reported. Abuses perpetrated by child soldiers will require rehabilitative responses as opposed to retributive measures. We suggest that the causes and consequences of each conflict be examined separately in seeking to strike a balance between the implications of an amnesty and the goals of intergroup conflict resolution, national reconciliation and rehabilitation.

5.4 Responding to Physical Injury

Article 39 of the Convention on the Rights of the Child requires States to take all appropriate measures to promote the physical and psychological recovery and social re-integration of a child victim of armed conflict, 'in an environment which fosters the health, self-respect and dignity of the child'.

There is no reason to believe that the effectiveness of responsive programmes is diminished if they address all injured youth as one group, be they participants or victims. The psychosocial consequences of suffering a war-related injury might vary, however, depending on the person's status as victim or participant, and a child who volunteers to fight might react differently to a battle-related injury than a child forced to fight. The reception or reaction of the family or the community might also affect how an injured combatant copes with a handicap or injury. No studies appear to consider these issues, but investigators and agencies designing psychosocial programmes for former soldiers could usefully take them into account.

The psychosocial responses to physical injury should be addressed together with medical treatment. According to one Gaza psychiatrist, '[m]any of the active participants in the *intifada* are "proud" of their injuries, they see them as a medal testifying to their patriotism and bravery. Some of them however find it difficult to cope with their injuries or traumas.'[38]

A psychologist working with *intifada*-injured youth in a YMCA programme in the West Bank observed that many had derived a sense of belonging from participation in the *intifada*, but felt extremely isolated after being injured. Many regretted having been involved, since it reduced them to 'half-persons' at home as opposed to heroes in the community. Those who had been only minimally involved found adjustment especially difficult. This psychologist believes that youth passing through the YMCA's counselling and vocational training emerge finding strength in activities other than violence.[39]

5.5   Education and Training for Ex-Combatants

Given the limited or non-existent educational opportunities for child soldiers, education as part of a demobilization and reintegration package makes perfect sense. Unfortunately, the vast majority of those who have spent their school-age years as combatants are likely to be more concerned with earning-capacity once they hand over their guns.

For those still of school-age, like the estimated 8,000 Mozambican RENAMO boys, standard education programmes may be an option, provided their material needs can be met by their families. In 1986 the Ugandan

38   Dr. Eyad El-Sarraj, 'The Psycho-political state of the Palestinians before and after the Intifada', unpublished paper delivered at the Truman Institute for Peace, The Hebrew University, 20 Mar. 1988, pp.8-9.

39   Their initial reaction to the programme is not always receptive, however. The former director of the programme explained that Palestinian youth see themselves as leaders and reject the YMCA adults 'telling them what to do'. Some Palestinians reportedly believe the YMCA is a CIA front or a US-backed programme aiming to convert Palestinians to Christianity or brain-wash the struggle from their minds.

government estimated that some 3,000 children, among them some 500 girls, were still in the army. Former UNICEF-representative to Uganda, Cole Dodge, maintained that '[t]hey should go to civilian schools. When they reach maturity they can decide whether to take up a trade or profession, or whether to go for a career in the army.'[40] Dodge felt that primary schooling should be combined with skills training, and although many children had no known parents and apparently preferred to stay 'home' with the NRA, he believed that tracing might have helped identify and reunite some children with their relatives.[41] Another alternative would have been to keep the children in the army, while providing special training in basic literacy and skills, such as welding and carpentry.[42] Those in favour of this option claimed that the children had no families, did not want to leave, and that they 'represented a potential to improve the quality of the NRA as they matured with credentials of loyalty, service and motivation.'[43] Those who disagreed feared that the psychological damage suffered by the children might make them a volatile group, whose eventual dissatisfaction combined with continued status as soldiers could pose security risks for the new government. This pessimism does not seem to have been borne out by events, although no detailed follow-up has been undertaken.[44]

During the 1992 armed cease-fire in El Salvador, while FMLN troops were concentrated in 'verification centres' pending demobilization, intensive education programmes (primarily literacy training) were launched by a local university with international funding. The programme helped alleviate boredom in the camps, but several young combatants interviewed for this study claimed it achieved few meaningful results. The final demobilization package included scholarships for those over eighteen who tested at the university entrance level, entry into the National Civil Police for those with at least ninth grade equivalency, vocational or industrial skills training, or agricultural skills training.[45] For lack of prior education, all or most ex-FMLN combatants under eighteen will participate

40   Cole P. Dodge, 'Child Soldiers of Uganda: What Does the Future Hold?' *Cultural Survival Quarterly* vol.10, no.4, 1986, p.33.
41   Cole P. Dodge and Magne Raundalen, *Reaching Children in War: Sudan, Uganda and Mozambique*, Sigma Forlag, Norway, 1991, pp.54-5.
42   'Uganda: Land of the Child Soldier, A Summary Report', Center on War and the Child, Arkansas, 1987, p.2.
43   Cole P. Dodge and Magne Raundalen, *Reaching Children in War: Sudan, Uganda and Mozambique*, Sigma Forlag, Norway, 1991, p.55.
44   Ibid., p.56. It appears that no records were kept of children discharged from the armed forces.
45   A similar set of options will soon be made available to demobilized armed forces troops. We were unable to verify how many of the approximately 32,000 discharged soldiers were under eighteen years old.

in one of the two skills training programmes.[46] They should eventually be able to obtain credit to buy land or to invest in a small business venture, and can always choose to enrol in the public schools.[47]

Vocational training is also being offered in Liberia for former members of any of the armed groups. The Liberian Opportunities Industrialization Center (LOIC) enroled 300 former soldiers in a programme to begin in April 1993 offering training in carpentry, shoe-making, sewing and masonry. The majority are from 15-30 years old. Despite, or because of coerced recruitment by all armed groups and/or the factors that motivated some participants to join up, including fear, hunger, revenge for specific acts of violence, LOIC reports no apparent animosity between former members of different warring factions. The Silesian Brothers of Don Bosco run a similar vocational programme on a smaller scale for younger street children, many of whom have participated in the fighting. Both programmes pre-date the conflict and are being adapted to address the needs of former soldiers.

The child's right to education in a situation of conflict raises a number of very practical questions relating to *responsibility*. Article 28 of the Convention on the Rights of the Child recognizes the right of the child to education, and obliges States parties to take various steps to ensure that the right is achieved 'progressively and on the basis of equal opportunity.' International obligations apply to the totality of a State's territory, but in time of conflict the authorities may lose control over particular areas. In such circumstances, the State's non-compliance may be excused if it can show, in effect, that it has done the best in the circumstances. The question then is whether an alternative obligation falls upon the non-government entity actually exercising control. Although responsibility in certain cases does attach to control over territory, education is not clearly covered, and may be practically unachievable during the initial stages of armed insurrection where the party in control lacks infrastructure and resources.

---

46   An attempt to collect statistics on the education level of FMLN troops was made when they entered the 'verification centres' in early 1992. 60.58% refused to reply and of the remainder: 12.67% had no formal education, 22.69% had some primary education, 2.99% had some secondary education, 1.07% had some university-level education. Statistics correlating age with education were unavailable.

47   Legislation enabling ex-FMLN and ex-armed forces troops who were sixteen years old at 1 Feb. 1992 to acquire credit is currently being drafted. It is unclear what provisions will be made for the 526 FMLN ex-combatants between 11-15 years old.

5.6 Additional Considerations

In designing and implementing programmes, the moment of intervention must be chosen carefully. Action taken during transition, for example, might facilitate demobilization and reintegration. Policies or programmes that offer incentives for child soldiers to demobilize are essential in themselves. Chapter 2 suggests why a youth who takes up a gun may hesitate to give it up: the gun may be the only way to get basic necessities, such as clothes, food, or housing; or demobilization may carry the risk of rejection by one's family or community, and a return to poverty or persecution. Incentives to demobilize and concrete programmes oriented to facilitate the transition to civilian life might also reduce the rise in delinquency and dissatisfaction that occurs when many wars cease. NGOs and international agencies can help to reduce this threat by insisting on full disarming of all troops and providing means of employment or income for ex-combatants. In instances of delinquency by former combatants, local agencies should consider the special psychosocial needs of such offenders. Here, research that helps to predict possible disciplinary problems might be useful, together with programmes to assist teachers and parents anticipate, understand and cope with disruptive youth.

6

Developing the Protection of
Child Soldiers: The Uses of
Law and Process

Linda Miller
Morazan, El Salvador, 1989. Young FMLN soldier.

Yann Gamblin – UNICEF
Uganda, 1986. Mukamba, 9 years old, known for his marksmanship.

THE PRECEDING CHAPTERS HAVE ILLUSTRATED both the extent of the problem of child soldiers, and the difficulties in the way of improving protection of children and bringing to an end the practices of child recruitment and participation. The law is not always as clear or as helpful as it might be, and there is an unfortunate tension between legislation, on the one hand, and the practices of governments and non-governmental entities (NGEs), on the other. All areas of the law need upgrading. A significant part of international human rights law is based on the protection of children and young persons up to the age of 18, and this general principle should be central to the interpretation of Additional Protocols I and II and the Convention on the Rights of the Child. So far as recruitment is concerned, however, universal and formal acceptance of 18 as the minimum age is a key objective, and ways to achieve this end are suggested below.

A rule that prohibits recruitment might meet part of the problem, but participation is not likely to cease only on that account, because of the practical reasons outlined in Chapter 2 and the legal short-comings described in Chapter 3. The present chapter suggests how to develop the range of standards applicable, in particular, to internal strife and 'low-level' disturbances. In this connection, human rights law and customary international law, which is binding on States apart from treaties, can help to bridge the gap between established rules and desirable standards.

Moving from law to process, section 2 briefly describes the human rights mechanisms available at regional and universal level. These are some of the avenues that might be used to act on human rights violations confronting child soldiers, or to contribute to the development of rules and standards. Often, they are open to non-governmental organizations, whose only interest need lie in achieving the protection guaranteed by the treaty in question.

Section 3 considers non-legal methods, to be used in parallel with formal processes, to bring about change in law and practice, but also to pressure those who violate children's human rights by recruiting them as soldiers or allowing their participation in conflict.

Finally, section 4 identifies the sort of information needed by advocates for children, and where it can be found, and briefly considers how the system of protection can be accessed.

6.1 Developing the Law

6.1.1 International Humanitarian Law

Despite numerous provisions oriented to the protection of children in armed conflict, international humanitarian law, up to its most recent reformulation in 1977, makes an exception of young persons between the ages of 15 and 18—either because it expressly permits their occasionally graduated recruitment; or because it fails to draw the line against their participation. Even though most States today have adopted 18 as the minimum age for compulsory recruitment and the exercise of other critical civic duties, such as voting, in time of conflict the attraction of children as combatants or 'participants' is likely to reassert itself.

International humanitarian law provides the basis for a rule of non-recruitment and non-participation, but it needs updating and clarifying. No formal revision of the Additional Protocols or the Geneva Conventions can be expected in the near future, and the process of change must therefore be led from the grass roots, through national Red Cross and Red Crescent Societies, with the endorsement of the Council of Delegates and, hopefully, the 26th International Conference. It must be driven, too, by non-governmental organizations of all persuasions, using the resources of government, parliament, regional and international organizations, the media and public support.

The reasons of practice and principle for such a change have been set out above, and specific arguments follow. Ideally, at this stage the objectives should include,

- adoption in national legislation and practice of 18 as the minimum age for recruitment or participation, directly or indirectly, in armed conflict or related activities (such as policing or riot control)
- unilateral declarations, interpreting article 38 of the Convention on the Rights of the Child, as well as the relevant provisions of Additional Protocols I and II, recognizing 18 as the minimum age
- formal endorsement by the International Committee of the Red Cross and the International Red Cross and Red Crescent movement of minimum age 18
- development of a protocol in an appropriate forum, to include the principle of non-recruitment/non-participation of persons under 18, and to develop generally the standards of protection of children and young persons in armed conflict and violent internal strife

6.1.2 International Law and Internal Strife

With 'low-level' internal conflict now the dominant form of armed struggle, a significant cause of the problems facing children and young persons lies in the perceived non-applicability of international humanitarian law (the so-called threshold issue),[1] or the inherent weaknesses of the international system for the protection of human rights, including the non-ratification of treaties, inadequate international oversight, the scope for derogation in time of 'national emergency', and the lack of recourse.

Theodor Meron and others, including rapporteurs and working groups within the United Nations system, have clearly identified the types of violations frequently occurring in violent internal strife and not yet effectively addressed by international rules and standards:[2] summary and arbitrary execution; torture and inhumane treatment; disappearances; hostage-taking; terror and intimidation of civilian populations; deportation and forced relocation; abuse or lack of judicial process; large-scale and prolonged administrative detention; and collective punishment.

Children are as likely to be affected by these abuses as anyone else, but it may be that by concentrating on the special protection due to children because of their age and vulnerability, an overall improvement in standards can best be secured. Meron proposes a declaration, to apply to 'all situations involving substantial and protracted acts of violence,' and to 'all persons present in the State'. In order to avoid the potentially prejudicial distinctions mentioned above, such as have affected 'conflict', 'combatant', 'civilian', 'participant' and 'non-combatant', he proposes a generally applicable standard of humane treatment, buttressed with specific prohibitions on the use of disproportionate force, or the use of weapons calculated to cause unnecessary or indiscriminate suffering, 'against children, peaceful demonstrators and other defenceless persons.'[3] So far as it deals specifically

---

1   The 25th International Conference of the Red Cross, in its resolution on Respect for International Humanitarian law in Armed Conflicts and Action by the ICRC for Persons Protected by the Geneva Conventions highlighted violations of the GCs and 'a disturbing decline in the respect for international humanitarian law'; it acknowledged that 'disputes about the legal classification of conflicts too often hinder the implementation of international humanitarian law': Doc. P.2/CI, Ann. 1 (1986).

2   Meron, Theodor, 'On the Inadequate Reach of Humanitarian and Human Rights Law and the Need for a New Instrument,' 77 *Am. J. Int'l. Law* 589 (1983); 'Towards a Humanitarian Declaration on Internal Strife,' 78 *Am. J. Int'l. Law* 859 (1984); *Human Rights in Internal Strife: Their International Protection*, Hersch Lauterpacht Memorial Lectures, Cambridge, 1987; 'Draft Model Declaration on Internal Strife,' *International Review of the Red Cross*, Jan.-Feb. 1988, 59; 'ICRC Protection and Assistance Activities in Situations not Covered by International Humanitarian Law,' ibid., 9-37; Gasser, Hans-Peter, 'A Measure of Humanity in Internal Disturbances and Tensions: Proposal for a Code of Conduct,' ibid., 38. See also Turku/Åbo Declaration, 1990.

3   Cf. para. (c), commentary to art. 3, UN Code of Conduct for Law Enforcement Officials, adopted by UNGA res. 34/169, 17 Dec. 1979.

with the rights of the child, however, the Draft Declaration is content to reiterate age 15 as the minimum for recruitment or participation.[4] The 1990 Declaration of Minimum Humanitarian Standards, adopted by an expert meeting in Turku/Åbo, Finland, moves ahead in recommending that, 'All efforts shall be made not to allow persons below the age of eighteen to take part in acts of violence.'[5]

Although the idea of a declaration of minimum standards for application in situations of internal strife has come to the notice of the UN General Assembly,[6] its adoption by States is currently stalled. In addition, the ICRC itself has inclined away from a formal legal instrument, partly because of concerns about counter-arguments based on sovereignty, in favour of a Code of Conduct framed in ordinary language:

> Children, particularly if deprived of their liberty, shall be accorded the respect due to them on account of their age. They must never be compelled or encouraged to take part in acts of violence.[7]

There are practical considerations on all sides of the code-declaration-protocol debate. A declaration on minimum standards for application in situations of internal strife, adopted in a broad forum such as the United Nations General Assembly, would help to resolve any doubts regarding the scope of international law. Provided it is revised to incorporate the protection of children and youth up to 18 from recruitment and participation in conflict, this initiative should be supported by national groups vis-à-vis their own governments.

6.2   International Implementation

6.2.1 International Organizations

The human rights machinery includes the formal procedures for submission of complaints to supervisory or review bodies, and also the various international organizations having responsibilities in the broad field in which child soldiers are engaged. Some, such as the United Nations Security Council or the General Assembly, operate at a high political level where

---

4   Draft Declaration, art. 8.

5   1990 Declaration of Minimum Humanitarian Standards, art. 10; Institute for Human Rights, Åbo Akademi University, Turku/Åbo, Finland, 1991.

6   Cf. UN doc. E/CN.4/Sub.2/1991/55.

7   See Gasser, above note 2, 51-8. Rule 12 of the Draft Code of Conduct. The draft code does not define 'children' or deal with voluntary participation.

specific human rights issues come relatively infrequently, and generally only after action taken in another part of the system. The Economic and Social Council (ECOSOC) is also somewhat remote from actual violations, so that children's rights advocates are likely to find more immediate attention in other fora. Nevertheless, the United Nations as a whole is necessarily bound by article 1 of the UN Charter, to pursue the purposes and principles of the organization; and by article 55, to promote 'universal respect for, and observance of, human rights and fundamental freedoms for all without distinction as to race, sex, language, or religion.'

The *Commission on Human Rights*,[8] an organ of ECOSOC, meets annually in Geneva. It now comprises fifty-three member States, and many other States and over one hundred non-governmental organizations participate in its work. Its mandate today includes the protection of minorities, the prevention of discrimination, and 'any other matter concerning human rights ...' ECOSOC resolutions 1235 and 1503, adopted in 1967 and 1970 respectively, have widened the Commission's terms of reference to allow it to deal with gross violations of human rights. The '1503 procedure', in Philip Alston's words, is a form of 'petition-information system';[9] it offers no redress to individuals, but by bringing complaints to the notice of the Commission, helps it to identify situations involving 'a consistent pattern of gross and reliably attested violations'; it is not a rapid process, however, and operates in a highly political environment. The '1235 procedure' provides the basis for the Commission's annual public debate on gross violations of human rights,[10] which in turn allows various methods of investigation of human rights practices, including fact-finding, and for corresponding pressure on offending States. Again, however, it is slow and its overall effectiveness must be judged accordingly.

The *Sub-Commission on Prevention of Discrimination and Protection of Minorities*[11] is a body of twenty-six independent experts, elected in their individual capacities by the Commission on Human Rights. A principal role is to provide advice to the latter, and it has come to play a pivotal role as a 'link between the official, intergovernmental institutions and the general public, as represented by the NGOs.'[12] The mandate of the Sub-Commission extends not only to the subject-matter of its name, but also to any other function entrusted to it by either the Commission or ECOSOC. It produces

8   See Alston, P., 'The Commission on Human Rights,' in Alston, P., ed., *The United Nations and Human Rights: A Critical Appraisal*, 1992, 126-210.
9   Ibid., p. 146.
10   Ibid., p. 155.
11   See Eide, A., 'The Sub-Commission on Prevention of Discrimination and Protection of Minorities,' in Alston, P., ed., *United Nations and Human Rights*, 211-64.
12   Ibid., p. 211.

studies, for example, on child labour, discrimination against indigenous populations, or slavery; uses semi-permanent working groups, for example, on detention; debates issues; contributes to standard-setting; monitors implementation and responds to alleged violations of human rights. NGOs play an important role as sources of information and in bringing such issues before the Sub-Commission, so that consistent patterns of human rights violations ideally can be brought to the attention of the Commission itself. A recent Sub-Commission resolution exhorted the government of Guatemala to ensure respect for human rights and international humanitarian law and to abolish the civil patrol system.[13]

The *Office of the United Nations High Commissioner for Refugees (UNHCR)* has the responsibility to provide international protection to refugees, and supervisory functions with respect to the 1951 Convention and 1967 Protocol relating to the Status of Refugees. Neither instrument deals specifically with the problems of recruitment or participation of children in conflict, but UNHCR has intervened with governments to ensure that refugee camps and settlements are located away from borders, to avert the possibility of armed attacks, but also to maintain the civilian character of such camps, precisely so that they do not become centres of recruitment either for adults or for children and young persons.[14]

UNHCR's general protection function draws on its human rights competence with respect to refugees, and it has specifically recognized its responsibilities towards refugee children whose human rights, as described above, may be violated by governments and non-governmental entities seeking to recruit them. Like the ICRC, the remedies available to UNHCR are relatively limited, often to diplomatic interventions with governments. The Office reports regularly to its Executive Committee, however, which has repeatedly condemned forced recruitment and participation in conflict. As a subsidiary organ of the UN General Assembly, it may provide expert advice to the Committee on the Rights of the Child on issues within its mandate. The High Commissioner's reports are thus one, somewhat protracted and rather remote way in which the problem of refugee children subject to recruitment or participation in conflict can be brought to the attention of a wider forum. UNHCR's strength as a human rights mechanism lies perhaps in the fact that it is widely represented throughout the world, and particularly in areas of conflict that not only involve child soldiers, but also refugee flows. Its contacts with governments and non-government entities can thus help it to influence policy and practice in favour of

13   *Situation of Human Rights in Guatemala*, UN doc. Res. 1992/18, E/CN.4/1993/2, E/CN.4/Sub.2/1992/58 at 54-56.
14   See above, chapter 3, section 3.3.3.

protecting refugee children from recruitment and participation; such a role should be central to its international responsibilities.

Finally, *UNICEF, the United Nations Fund for Children*, has very specific responsibilities for mothers and children, at all times and particularly in times of conflict when the need for special care and protection are most pronounced. Even though UNICEF has no supervisory functions, article 45 of the Convention on the Rights of the Child authorises it to provide expert advice and to submit reports to the Committee with regard to Convention implementation in specific countries. UNICEF should consider developing guidelines for monitoring implementation, and encouraging local NGOs to become involved in monitoring and informing the Committee. UNICEF's active involvement at field and programme level place staff in a position to influence both governments and non-governmental entities to cease or avoid recruiting children or using them in combat.

Each of the above organizations ought in principle to have child soldiers within their mandate. At its Third Session in January 1993, for example, the Committee on the Rights of the Child requested the Special Rapporteur on former Yugoslavia to take the Convention on the Rights of the Child fully into consideration when carrying out his mandate and preparing future reports.[15] Whether rapporteurs and working groups are able to do anything in a particular case will often depend, not only on the political dimensions to the issue and the way in which it is presented, but also upon the organizations being presented with accurate and reliable information relating to recruiting practices; these matters are dealt with below.

6.2.2 International Committee of the Red Cross

The *International Committee of the Red Cross (ICRC)* is an obvious first avenue of complaint, wherever a party to a conflict appears to be acting in violation of its obligations under the Geneva Conventions and/or the Additional Protocols.

The ICRC may take action on its own initiative, or on receipt of complaints, the principle motivation being 'essentially one criterion...the interest of the victims whom its mandate requires it to protect and assist.'[16] The ICRC is not like other supervisory bodies, however, and due regard must be given to the limitations imposed by the standards of neutrality, impartiality and independence, as well as the inadequacies of existing

---

15 Committee on the Rights of the Child, Report on the Third Session: UN doc. CRC/C/16, 2 Mar. 1993, para. 180.

16 'Action by the International Committee of the Red Cross in the Event of Breaches of International Humanitarian Law,' *International Review of the Red Cross*, Mar.-Apr. 1981, 1-8.

procedures. This often means that the ICRC can only take up issues diplomatically and confidentially, although it reserves the right of 'going public' in appropriate circumstances, for example, when

- the violations are major and repeated
- the steps taken confidentially have not succeeded in putting an end to the violations
- such publicity is in the interest of the persons or populations affected or threatened
- the ICRC delegates have witnessed the violations with their own eyes, or the existence and extent of those breaches were established by reliable and verifiable sources.[17]

6.2.2.1 Violations of International Humanitarian Law

International humanitarian law offers a variety of different measures for dealing with breaches.[18] Article 90 of Additional Protocol I, for example, provides for the establishment of an International Fact-Finding Commission, when twenty Parties have made the necessary declaration. The Commission, which came into being in 1992,[19] is competent to enquire into allegations by a participating State with respect to grave breaches or other serious violations of the Geneva Conventions and Additional Protocol I by any other participating State. It must thus wait to be seized of any matter, and is otherwise only able to begin an inquiry with the consent of all the parties to the conflict; at its first session, the Commission nevertheless offered its services in the investigation of all violations of humanitarian law, including those committed in civil conflict, subject to the consent of all the parties. Under the existing terms of reference, the Commission is limited to inquiry into the *facts*, and has no power to determine formally whether there has been a grave breach or serious violation.[20]

Traditionally, the system of international humanitarian law has relied heavily on national legal systems, in part using the principle of 'universal jurisdiction', in the sense that any State party is competent to try any person alleged to have violated the obligations in question. Grave breaches of the laws of war are war crimes, and the Geneva Conventions oblige States

---

17 Ibid., p. 6.

18 See generally, Thomson, J.F., 'Repression of Violations,' 9 *Aust. YB. Int'l Law* 325 (1985).

19 At 31 Dec. 1992, thirty-three States had made the declaration provided for under API, art. 90.

20 This will make rather difficult the second part of its mandate, namely, to 'facilitate, through its good offices, the restoration of an attitude of respect' for the Conventions and Protocol I: art. 90.2(c)(i). The IFFC shall report its findings of fact to the Parties (art. 90.5) with appropriate recommendations; but may not report publicly, unless all the Parties to the conflict have requested it to do so: art. 90.5(c).

parties to search for and try those alleged to have committed or ordered the commission of 'grave breaches', including wilful killing and torture or inhumane treatment.[21] Such a universal right to prosecute, however, only applies to the 'grave breaches'; States parties are required to take the 'necessary' measures for the suppression of all other acts contrary to the Conventions. It is doubtful whether such provisions improve the protection of the child soldier in time of international armed conflict,[22] and in internal conflict the situation is even less secure. States are frequently unwilling to prosecute their own nationals, while Additional Protocol II contains no international enforcement mechanism at all. In these circumstances, domestic and international public opinion, as well as diplomatic interventions, may be the first line of recourse. Conscious of these limitations and the non-functioning system of Protecting Powers, Hans-Peter Gasser has nonetheless explained how the ICRC's protection activities can contribute to a measure of indirect supervision:[23]

> For example, one object of a visit to a place of detention is to check that the pertinent provisions of the Geneva Conventions are being respected. It is also obvious that scrupulous respect for the Geneva Conventions is a constitutive and essential element of effective protection. ICRC action in protecting war victims is thus necessarily and organically linked to checking that humanitarian law is respected.

The combination of the mandate to protect and assist the victims of war with the right of humanitarian initiative gives the ICRC a potentially valuable and influential role in combatting the recruitment and participation of child soldiers, even if specific action may depend upon the agreement of the parties concerned. The practice whereby the ICRC would forward complaints of breaches of international humanitarian law to the party concerned did not prove effective,[24] but the receipt of reliable information on such practices will clearly help the ICRC to fulfil its mandate.

---

21 See further, arts. 50, 51, 130 and 147 of the First, Second, Third and Fourth Geneva Conventions, respectively; also API, arts. 11 and 85.

22 Note however API, art. 87, which obliges governments to ensure that their military commanders are instructed to prevent and suppress breaches. Once aware of an actual or imminent breach, commanders must initiate action to prevent such breach, or to take disciplinary or penal action against the offenders. States parties are obliged to provide instruction in humanitarian law; see arts. 47, 48, 127, and 144 of the four Geneva Conventions, respectively; API, art. 83; APII, art. 19.

23 H.-P. Gasser, 'Scrutiny,' 9 *Aust. YB Int'l Law* 345, 355-6 (1985).

24 The practice was abandoned because of States' unwillingness to act upon such communications; see above note 23.

6.2.3 Universal Treaty Monitoring Bodies

The present section gives a brief overview of some of the different treaty monitoring bodies operating within the United Nations system, which may have child soldiers within their mandate.[25]

The *Human Rights Committee*[26] was established in 1976 to monitor the application of the 1966 Covenant on Civil and Political Rights and its Optional Protocol. It comprises eighteen experts, elected for a four-year term by over one hundred and ten States which have now ratified that treaty, and meets twice a year. Its principal functions are to consider reports from States Parties and, for those States which have opted accordingly, to hear complaints against them. The complaints procedure takes two forms: inter-State 'communications', under the Covenant itself; and individual 'communications' under the Optional Protocol.

Reports are due periodically from States Parties on the measures taken to implement the Covenant at the national level, which are then examined by the Committee in the presence of State representatives; countries in which conflict is taking place can be specifically questioned with respect to the measures, if any, being taken to protect children. The Committee has also adopted the practice of issuing 'General Comments,' giving its own understanding of how articles of the Covenant are to be interpreted.[27] The inter-State complaints procedure is in force, but unused, and the individual procedure under the Optional Protocol has become the Committee's second principal activity. The process is relatively simple, and similar in its basic criteria to other review systems. If claims are 'admissible', the Committee examines them on the merits and forwards its non-binding 'views' to the State party and the individual concerned; although the merits are considered in private, the 'views' are published. A communication will be admissible, if it concerns one of the rights and freedoms in the Covenant and is not anonymous; all domestic remedies, if available, must have been exhausted and the same matter must not be under consideration in another international procedure.[28] It is *not* necessary that the author of the communication also be the alleged victim of the human rights violation; an authorised

25   For more detailed information, see Alston, Philip, ed., *The United Nations and Human Rights: A Critical Appraisal*, 1992.

26   See Opsahl, T., 'The Human Rights Committee,' in Alston, P., *United Nations and Human Rights*, 369-443; for a more detailed treatment, see McGoldrick, D., *The Human Rights Committee: Its Role in the Development of the International Covenant on Civil and Political Rights*, 1991.

27   With respect to art. 24 of the Covenant, the Committee drew attention to the need for States to include in their reports information on measures adopted to ensure that children do not take a direct part in armed conflicts; see General Comments: UN doc. CCPR/C/21/Rev.1, 19 May 1989, p.22, para. 3.

28   Opsahl, above note 26, pp. 423-6. Child advocates will therefore need to ensure co-ordination of effort.

representative, lawyer or other person having a sufficient link may suffice, when it appears that the persons concerned cannot act on their own behalf.[29]

The *Committee on Economic, Social and Cultural Rights*, which held its first session in 1987, is the successor to 'eight years of thoroughly inefficient monitoring by a succession of Working Groups...' set up by ECOSOC.[30] Like its civil and political rights counterpart, the Committee comprises eighteen members elected, not under the Covenant, but under the authority of ECOSOC; and its mandate is precisely to assist ECOSOC to do its job, rather than having direct supervisory responsibilities in its own right. In this sense of its mandate, the Committee seeks to clarify the content of the Covenant on Economic, Social and Cultural Rights, examine State reports, draft general interpretative comments, and become an effective monitoring system.

The *Committee on Torture*, set up under article 17 of the 1984 United Nations Convention against Torture and other Cruel, Inhuman or Degrading Treatment or Punishment to monitor implementation, is composed of ten experts elected by States parties to serve in their personal capacity.[31] States ratifying this convention must accept a reporting obligation. Two optional procedures are also provided, one allowing the Committee to consider individual complaints, and the other allowing for inter-State complaints.[32]

Uniquely, the Committee against Torture also has the power to investigate cases on its own initiative, where it receives 'reliable information which appears to it to contain well-founded indications that torture is being systematically practised *in the territory* of a State party.'[33] Although this too is an optional procedure, States have to *opt out* of the article 20 process under article 28. As one of the newest review committees, the Committee against Torture also makes somewhat greater provision for the formal involvement of NGOs in its proceedings; like individual complainants, NGOs are likely to be one of the best sources of information, particularly for the article 20 procedure.

Last, and by no means least, is the *Committee on the Rights of the Child*. Composed of ten independent members, the committee's mandate is similar

---

29   Ibid., p. 424.
30   See Alston, P., 'The Committee on Economic, Social and Cultural Rights,' in Alston, P., *The United Nations and Human Rights*, 473-508.
31   See Byrnes, Andrew, 'The Committee against Torture,' in Alston, P., ed., *United Nations and Human Rights*, 509-46.
32   Ibid., pp. 523-4.
33   Art. 20(1), 1984 Convention against Torture; emphasis supplied. The reference 'in the territory of a State' might open the way to investigation of the activities of non-governmental entities, subject to an appropriate interpretation of the torture definition in art. 1, which talks of actions of officials or people in authority.

to those described above, including the examination of country reports on measures taken to implement the provisions of the 1989 Convention on the Rights of the Child; and like other committees, it is already facing the problem of large numbers of outstanding reports.

The Committee on the Rights of the Child is nevertheless likely to be one of the most important mechanisms in the struggle against the recruitment of child soldiers and the participation of children in conflict. It too has so far shown itself open to NGOs, allowing them in its first sessions to speak from the floor. The Committee is establishing procedures for urgent action on behalf of children, where there is reliable information of a non-political character, indicating a serious situation involving the risk of further rights violations. At its second session, in Geneva from 28 September - 9 October 1992, the Committee spent a whole day discussing the question of children in armed conflict. Various suggestions were made, including the drafting of a general comment on child recruitment and the development of an optional protocol establishing minimum age 18 as the rule for recruitment and participation.[34] At its third session, from 11-29 January 1993, the Committee recommended to the General Assembly that 'a major United Nations study' should be undertaken of the serious problem of children in armed conflict. It also decided to entrust one of its members with preparing a preliminary draft of an optional protocol to the Convention on the Rights of the Child, raising the minimum age of recruitment to 18.[35]

6.2.4 Regional Treaty Monitoring Bodies

Both the European and the American conventions on human rights provide for supervisory and petitions procedures at individual and State level. The *European Commission on Human Rights* and the *European Court of Human Rights* are the principle investigatory and adjudicatory organs in Europe, with certain responsibilities also shared by the Committee of Ministers. Claims may be brought by States, individuals or groups, but neither the 1950 European Convention nor its subsequent protocols deal directly with child soldiers and children's rights at large are rather undeveloped. A complaint involving recruitment or participation will need to be framed, therefore, with due regard to related rights or freedoms, such as the right to be treated with dignity and respect, and the prohibition on cruel, inhuman or degrading treatment. The inherent limitations of this approach can be seen in the European Commission's rejection of claims against the United

34   Committee on the Rights of the Child, Report on the Second Session: UN doc. CRC/C/10. 19 Oct. 1992, paras. 61-77.
35   Committee on the Rights of the Child, Report on the Third Session: UN doc. CRC/C/16, 2 Mar. 1993, paras. 151-2, 176, Annex VII.

Kingdom by boy soldiers and sailors in the late 1960s.[36] The applicants had joined the armed forces with parental consent at the age of 15 or 16, for a nine year term to be counted from their eighteenth birthday; for various reasons, they had each applied unsuccessfully for discharge. The European Commission held that their applications were 'manifestly ill-founded', ruling that military service could not be considered as forced labour, given the terms of article 4(3)(b) of the Convention; that the young age of the applicants was insufficient alone to establish a condition of servitude; that an application to be discharged did not involve a 'civil right' within the meaning of article 6; and that family life, protected in principle by article 8, could not be so broadly interpreted as to cover them. United Kingdom law and practice were nevertheless amended in light of the controversy surrounding these cases, and it is possible that the European Commission would decide them differently today.

The 1969 American Convention on Human Rights provides for the *Inter-American Court of Human Rights* and continues the role of the *Inter-American Commission on Human Rights*, which had already exercised certain responsibilities under the earlier American Declaration of the Rights of Man. The general approach of these institutions is similar to that of the European models. The Commission recently heard the case of a young Guatemalan forcibly conscripted into the military, which puts in issue both the practice of systematic forced recruitment and the State's failure to respond or to provide domestic remedies.[37]

The *African Commission on Human and People's Rights* held its twelfth session in the Gambia from 12-21 October 1992. In private sessions, it examined a large number of communications concerning gross violations of human rights. The 1990 African Charter on the Rights and Welfare of the Child, not yet in force, provides for the establishment of an African Committee of Experts to promote the rights of the child, monitor implementation and ensure protection, and interpret the treaty's provisions.[38] States are to report on their measures of implementation, and the Committee 'may receive communications from any group or non-governmental organization recognized by the Organization for African Unity or the United Nations relating to any matter covered by [the] Charter.' Moreover, the Committee has the power to investigate alleged violations.[39]

36 Applications 3435-3438/67: 28 *Collections of Decisions* 109-31.

37 *The Law Group Docket*, publication of the International Human Rights Law Group, Wash. DC, vol.7, no.2, Dec. 1992 at 7.

38 Art. 42, African Charter on the Rights and Welfare of the Child, adopted by the Twenty-Sixth Ordinary Session of the Assembly of Heads of State and Government of the Organization of African Unity, 3-7 July 1990, Addis Ababa, Ethiopia.

39 Arts. 44 and 45.

6.3   Politics and Pressure

Human rights mechanisms are one formal way in which to bring the violations of children's rights to the attention of international supervisory or adjudicatory bodies. Although their influence can be considerable, the procedures tend to be protracted and the actual recruitment of children and young persons or their participation in conflict may not fit easily within traditional descriptions or interpretations of rights. For example, the treatment of children in such situations does not necessarily amount to torture, and in the particular circumstances of a conflict, may not amount to cruel or inhuman treatment. Much depends on the facts, and while children detained as prisoners of war or for reasons related to conflict may well raise issues under the Torture Convention, to argue for the involvement of the Committee on Torture in all cases can be counter-productive.

Other fundamental weaknesses of both human rights and humanitarian law mechanisms are their inability to reach NGEs and their lack of an effective fact-finding capacity, a feature of international adjudication that reflects traditional conceptions of sovereignty and non-intervention. Particularly close attention must be paid, therefore, to the preparation and presentation of claims.

The 'political' dimensions to certain human rights fora have been mentioned above. This factor is not necessarily to be regretted, let alone avoidable, for many practices leading to violations of human rights are political in origin, and will be political in solution. What it does mean, however, is that action to combat child recruitment must also be pursued in political bodies, in order to bring the necessary pressure on those responsible, and above all to deal with the systemic or root causes that lead children to take up arms. Discussion and investigation must be promoted in international fora, for example, in the substantive and subsidiary organs of the United Nations system, in regional commissions and regional organizations, such as the Organization of African Unity, the Organization of American States and the Council of Europe. Acceptance of certain basic human values, including the principle of non-recruitment and non-participation, can be clarified as essential conditions of membership in such organizations, thus bringing home the message that those seeking recognition and 'legitimacy' through armed conflict already have international responsibilities.

At the national level, certain governments are beginning to link development and other assistance to compliance with human rights standards. The *conditionality* of aid can be promoted by non-governmental organizations in relations with their national governments. The practice of under-age recruitment should be recognized as an obstacle of principle to economic assistance and to many levels of co-operation. This in turn means that policy-makers must be sensitized to what is going on in different countries, through informed debate in Parliament, in the media, and through non-governmental organizations. Public opinion can be a major driving force in the campaign against child soldiers; the media too must be told what is going on, and encouraged to undertake in-depth reporting and analysis of such situations for the broadest dissemination.

There is also considerable scope for international support for local initiatives. Non-governmental organizations, again, are often in a position to assist in the development of grass-roots initiatives geared to local solutions for the problems of recruitment and participation, including legal processes and the implementation of programmes of response. As clearly indicated above, however, measures to prevent recruitment and participation must go beyond rules and criticism of practice, to reach the causes and provide effective alternatives. Non-governmental assistance could be especially fruitful, nevertheless, in marshalling a broad, cross-regional approach to practices in a particular country, or in covering the full spectrum of human rights monitoring and investigating institutions.

6.4 Information and Application

6.4.1 Knowing the Law

The four Geneva Conventions require States parties to disseminate the texts as widely as possible, in peace and in war; the study of the Conventions is to be included in military instruction programmes and, if possible, in civilian programmes, 'so that the principles...may become known to all their armed forces and to the entire population.'[40] The objective of dissemination was endorsed by the 1977 Diplomatic Conference, and has been frequently confirmed by the UN General Assembly.[41] If the primary role still falls upon States and governments, particularly where implementing legislation or instruction for regular armed forces are called for, the need and opportunities are much greater. The law must not only be known, it must

---

40   See arts. 47, 48, 127 and 144, respectively; and arts. 83 and 19 of the Additional Protocols.
41   See Meurant, J., 'Dissemination and Education,' 9 *Aust. YB Int'l Law* 364-73 (1985); Surbeck, J.J., 'Commentary,' ibid., 378-83.

be understood, assimilated and respected.[42] In much the same way, article 42 of the Convention on the Rights of the Child obliges States Parties 'to make the principles and provisions of the Convention widely known, by appropriate and active means, to adults and children alike.'

Although international humanitarian law can be complex, the core principles can be simply stated. In the present context, this means that no child or youth under eighteen should be required or allowed to participate in armed conflict, a general principle that finds ample additional support in human rights law. Dissemination of this basic standard, and of the various national, regional and international ways in which it can be promoted and protected, should be a regular feature of grass-roots programmes, for example, among National Red Cross and Red Crescent Societies, indigenous non-governmental organizations and other NGOs, as well as in the media.

6.4.2 Knowing the Facts

Promoting the basic principle of non-recruitment and non-participation and protecting the rights of children and child soldiers involves both knowing the law and knowing the facts. Like most administrative and quasi-judicial systems in the world, human rights machinery at national and international level depends on credible and trustworthy evidence as the basis for decisions. For advocates, this involves not just collecting accounts of events, but also ensuring the reliability of information, for example, by providing corroboration or evidence to show consistent patterns of behaviour on the part of governments or non-government entities.

Monitoring and reporting are areas in which co-operation among non-governmental organizations can compensate both for lack of resources, and for the daunting breadth of human rights concerns. By focusing on rights issues relevant to child soldiers, advocates can work towards achieving a coherent, consistent and accurate record of practice and violations. Standards already exist in the human rights field for the collection, recording and dissemination of information. Common terminology in the use of index terms or keywords is being developed rapidly across major language groups, so bridging the communication gap while also facilitating rapid access to stored data.

There is a strong case for the development of a database on the recruitment, conscription and participation of children and youth in armed conflict. Such a resource might be managed and maintained by an

---

42   Jäckli, R., 'What Does the Future hold for International Humanitarian Law?' 9 *Aust. YB Int'l Law* 384, 385 (1985).

independent non-governmental organization, operating within a wider international network. Information relating to child soldiers, such as reports on the practice of governments and non-government entities, could be shared on a network basis, thereby encouraging the development of cross-regional and cross-institutional strategies; and treated and stored for access and analysis by all concerned, either electronically or through a regular document dissemination or exchange facility. The advantages of centralizing information, understood in a non-exclusive and non-monopolistic sense, include the concentration of resources that can be brought to bear upon the data, and the real possibilities in assisting local initiatives, such as legal challenges or submissions to regional, political and supervisory institutions. A strong information base can also contribute effectively to the promotional aspects of the struggle on behalf of children involved in conflict, for example, by providing a credible resource for the media.

Regional networks are already beginning to form, for example, in Latin America, and are developing and adapting children's rights monitoring guidelines to the local context and needs, in order to help NGOs and others standardize their data collection.

6.4.3 Accessing the System

Whether in submissions to legal or political bodies, or in presenting a case to the public, both the issues of principle and the facts must be clearly stated. Certain rules are straightforward: No child under 15 shall be recruited into the armed forces. This 'binds' States whether they have ratified the Geneva Conventions, the Additional Protocols, and the Convention on the Right of the Child, or not; for it is a rule of customary international law. The further principle that no child or youth up to the age of 18 shall be recruited or allowed to participate in conflict is also simply stated; even if its roots are a little less deep, it is supported by the general principles of international humanitarian law, and by the fundamental rules that govern the protection of the child. Of relevance also are the rules of international law that prohibit torture, cruel or inhumane treatment, and arbitrary detention, as well as the specific protection due to children under general conventions such as that on the rights of the child.

With the basic rules in mind, a fairly straightforward approach can be adopted to the presentation of individual cases or patterns of abuse of rights in legal and political fora, and to the media at national and international level. A simple model communication can be suggested, drawing on the experience of treaty monitoring bodies and non-governmental organizations involved in the promotion of human rights.[43] First, the author of the claim should identify themselves, whether as victim, representative, or other complainant such an NGO concerned with children's rights.[44] If the author is only indirectly involved, he or she should state the reasons for acting on behalf of the alleged victim, indicating why a communication cannot be submitted directly by the victim, and the reasons for believing that the victim would approve action on his or her behalf. Secondly, basic details of the victim should follow, with names, date of birth, nationality, address or whereabouts, if known. Thirdly, the communication should identify the State concerned, which rules of customary international law, international humanitarian law, human rights or other conventions appear to have been violated, the domestic remedies available and exhausted, if any, and details of any other international procedures that have been invoked. Finally, the claim should include detailed description of the facts, including dates, so as to show which authority or entity is involved in the recruitment or enlistment of child soldiers, or in the detention of children for reasons related to armed conflict and internal strife.

Local and international non-governmental organizations are well-placed to develop the practical tools for accessing available protection systems, and for sensitizing the media and the public to the needs of children in war. A measure of regionalization and internationalization can help to ensure that a high profile is given to those who violate the rights of children, and that appropriate political, legal and material pressure is brought to bear in every quarter.

---

43   See McGoldrick, Dominic, *The Human Rights Committee: Its Role in the Development of the International Covenant on Civil and Political Rights*, 1991, Appendix III, Model Communication under the Optional Protocol, at p. 529.
44   The drafters of art. 45 CRC intended that 'other competent bodies' should include NGOs; NGOs may therefore contribute expert advice on the CRC's implementation and the Committee welcomes such submissions.

7

Findings
&
Recommendations

THIS STUDY HAS BROADENED OUR own understanding of the reasons why children take up arms or are forced to fight, even as it has confirmed the complexity of the issue, at the levels of law, policy and programmes. This work is very much part of a process; we hope it is a step towards showing that something can be done to prevent children from taking up arms, and that it provides some ideas and suggestions for the development of responses to this tragic and avoidable phenomenon.

It is striking how many States in principle support the transition to adulthood at age eighteen. They do so not only with respect to political rights, such as voting, but also very much more widely, for example, with respect to the supreme sanction of the criminal law, the death penalty, both in time of war and peace. Clearly, those under 18, no matter their individual capacities, are generally presumed not to appreciate fully the nature of their actions, or the extent of their own responsibility. The idea of the child and youth as a person under 18 needing special protection, even if on a diminishing scale, thus enjoys a wide measure of support.

Given the essentially political dimension to armed conflict, this choice of eighteen as the moment of transition to adulthood is not unreasonable; on the contrary, it would seem wrong indeed to compel or allow those who cannot influence political decisions to take up arms, whether with or without parental consent.

Why Children participate in Armed Conflict

Despite the point of principle, however, more children and youth bear arms in internal armed conflict and violent strife than ever before. They are now or have been coerced into joining government armed forces, for example, in Burma, Guatemala, El Salvador, and Ethiopia; or opposition movements, as in Mozambique, Angola, Sri Lanka, and Sudan. Forced recruitment is practised because of shortages of soldiers, institutionalized discrimination against certain sectors of society, a perceived need to control the population, or ideological vigour. Some groups also have discovered that young, impressionable children can be turned into the fiercest fighters through brutalization, exposure to and involvement in violence.

But not all child participants are necessarily driven into conflict.

Sometimes, they are among the first to join; at other times, they may even be the initiators of violent strife. What moves them lies deep in the roots of conflict, in the social, economic and political issues defining their lives. No matter how overwhelming these may seem, only by dealing with the big questions are we liable ultimately to be able to help children and youth avoid participation in conflict and reclaim their entitlement.

The line between voluntary and coerced participation is fluid and uncertain. As outsiders especially, we can rarely know with confidence whether this or that child is really capable of 'volunteering' in the way we would accept of an adult. What has become clearer, though it is obvious in itself, is that children and youth are particularly susceptible to certain types of pressure coming from certain people. The vast majority of young soldiers are not so much coerced, as exposed to subtle manipulation that is even more difficult to eliminate than outright forced recruitment. Examining different situations first hand, and taking account of the experience of others, we rediscovered the importance of knowing just who is the child soldier in a given conflict. Only with that knowledge base can we begin to deal with the factors producing voluntary involvement.

Interviews and anecdotal evidence confirm that many young people voluntarily join armed groups because of what has happened to them personally. Where a child is at, intellectually and developmentally, influences his or her understanding of objective experiences, such as death, loss or other trauma, and therefore also the response to join an armed group. How they see things is influenced in turn by their social milieu, what has come to be called *children's ecologies*, and by *developmental processes*. Parents, families, peer groups, schools, religious communities and other community-based institutions, exert pressures or send messages that lead children to participate in hostilities. They have an impact also on how a youth values the very choice to participate. How communities 'value' the reasons for conflict, for example, in terms of social justice, religious fanaticism, ethnic purity, redress of historic wrongs, will be central to children's own perceptions. If violence is prevalent at any level of society, it may override rational decision-making processes or non-violent options for conflict resolution.

Peer pressure is especially persuasive. Hopelessness turns to rage, there is no future. The child is witness to the abuse or death of family, arrest and torture. The support is gone. Guilt combines with the desire for revenge, walks hand in hand with need and vulnerability. The weapons of war seem to offer an answer, or at least a better alternative.

Knowledge of these factors puts in question the extent of the child's evolving capacity to determine what is in his or her best interests, and casts doubt on the argument that children can or should exercise their right of free association or freedom of movement by joining an armed group. When we asked youth why they volunteered for combat, we learnt how often and how extensively they are influenced from within their community, or by factors they have little capacity to analyze.

These experiences suggest three possible areas for intervention: First, interventions which aim at structural reform, by improving or eliminating the structural causes of profoundly negative personal experiences; secondly, interventions aimed at youth's appraisals of participation as a means of effecting change; and thirdly, interventions that counter children's feelings of helplessness, vulnerability and frustration.

In fact, interventions to reduce volunteerism must be directed as much at children's ecologies as at the children themselves. Perhaps if the serious consequences of participation for child soldiers, their families and communities, were more widely known and understood, this might reduce the short-term pride in participation. What we saw, however, was that the immediate survival needs or the long-term political objectives of adults often outweigh concerns for child participants. An effective policy against youth recruitment must therefore take account of adult perceptions and values, nowhere more urgently than in the passing on of ethnic hatred from generation to generation. And ultimately, it is not only a question of making the child *feel* empowered or secure, but rather of actually improving his or her security or capacity to effect change without a gun. This in turn may require a focus not so much on the child soldier, as on governments that commit or sanction disappearances, torture, and repression.

Preventing Recruitment and Participation

The 1989 UN Convention on the Rights of the Child, already ratified by some 154 States, is rightly recognized as a critical milestone in the legal protection of children. Even if neither treaties nor laws are enough to bring child recruitment to an end, knowing the rules and principles can nevertheless help to organize strategies for prevention. It *is* relevant that States have formal, legal obligations with respect to a wide range of *human rights*, under *international humanitarian law*, and that even where they have ratified no treaty, they may be bound by the rules of *customary international law*.

The international law of the child must be understood and used *in context*. It operates *primarily* between States, and generally has only an indirect effect on non-State actors such as individuals, 'non-government entities' (NGEs) or other groups; this does not exclude the possibility of individual liability for breaches of the law, however, and does not rule out the critical use of legal standards in evaluating activities affecting the interests of the child. Children, whether victims or participants in armed conflicts, are protected and their liberties ensured, at least in theory, by international and national law.

Although the basic principles are clear enough, the specific provisions of international law regulating the recruitment and participation of children in armed conflict turn on a number of factors, including the type of conflict, ratification of or accession to the relevant treaties, and, with respect to certain types of international obligation, the status of the party recruiting or employing children in its ranks. Whether specific rules of international humanitarian law apply may thus depend on whether the State has ratified the Geneva Conventions or the Additional Protocols, and whether the conflict in question falls within one of five categories: traditional international armed conflicts; *Additional Protocol I* article 1(4) conflicts, in which the authority representing a people has made a declaration of intention to apply the Conventions and Protocols; *Additional Protocol II* article 1(1) conflicts, between a State and organized armed groups under responsible command; *Common Article 3* conflicts under the 1949 Conventions; and finally riots, internal disorder and tensions subject to national law, human rights law and minimum international law standards.

Unfortunately, no determining body, standard or internationally accepted method for characterizing conflicts exists, although recent United Nations action on the situation in former Yugoslavia suggests that such a humanitarian competence might well evolve.

For the time being, in an international armed conflict, the parties to the conflict are required to take 'all feasible measures' to ensure that children do not take a direct part in hostilities. Although some considered this insufficient, it seems to us that what is 'feasible' is that which is capable of being done and, by definition, whatever is under the jurisdiction and control of a party is *prima facie* capable of being done. The parties to the conflict are obliged, in particular, to 'refrain from recruiting' children under fifteen into their own forces; a clear example of what is *feasible*, because within the authority or competence of the party. It will always be 'feasible' for organized fighting forces to have a policy of non-recruitment of children, though not necessarily to ensure its implementation at every level, particularly in guerilla-style conflicts where children and young persons actively seek to participate. The simplicity of the principle leads us to believe that the real challenge is to give the broadest dissemination to humanitarian law principles, insist on their formal acceptance by all parties to conflict, promote alternatives to enlistment or participation, and clarify the legal implications for those engaged in hostilities.

The formal immunity of children from recruitment and 'involvement' in internal armed conflicts is stronger in *Additional Protocol II*, which provides that 'children who have not attained the age of fifteen years shall *neither* be recruited in the armed forces or groups *nor* allowed to take part in hostilities'. But in many of the conflicts examined, the elaborate protection of international humanitarian law was marginalized, often for 'technical' reasons. Hence the necessity for advocates to stress the customary international law nature of the rules relating to the conduct of hostilities and the protection of vulnerable groups such as children. We recognize the need for care in identifying those rules which are realistically applicable in time of conflict, and in distinguishing between the formal applicability of rules, and the consequences of breach. Even in the absence of judicial or 'enforcement' machinery, however, conduct contrary to customary international law can be characterised as illegal, resulting in pressure to conform.

Customary international law draws from humanitarian law, the law of human rights, the law of the child, and the practice of States. Among the basic rules now applying to international and internal conflicts, is that knowingly to allow or to require the participation in conflict of children under fifteen years of age is a violation of their human rights under customary international law, no matter that the child 'volunteers'. In principle, young persons between fifteen and eighteen years should also benefit from the rule requiring non-recruitment and non-participation. The exceptions recognized in the 1977 Additional Protocols and the 1989 Convention on the Rights of the Child must be interpreted in the light of State practice, which generally recognizes eighteen as the minimum age, and the guiding principle of the best interests of the child.

The general practice of States is not to conscript below the age of eighteen, and not to assign volunteers under eighteen to active service; the exceptions are not so extensive or of such a character as to de-rail the emergence of a rule of customary international law. The principle of protecting children and young persons from involvement in armed conflict thus supplements the traditional scope of international humanitarian law. Practical problems nevertheless remain: First, to ensure the effective implementation of obligations among both States and non-governmental entities; and second, to eliminate the factors that motivate children to seek entry into armed groups. The conflicts we have reviewed oppose precisely the reality of children under arms to the ideal of applied rules, and expose the limits of a rule-based approach in situations where there is simply no capacity for rehabilitation, accommodation or alternatives.

Prevention strategies must therefore reflect the many and complex ways in which children and adolescents come to participate in hostilities, dealing with the issues of the conflict, as well as the factors personal to the child. Among these strategies aiming to break the pattern of forced recruitment by government forces is legal action on behalf of youth forcibly conscripted.

Initiatives by government agencies, such as human rights offices and commissions, merit international recognition and technical support. Related promotional work is called for, such as translating constitutional provisions and legal entitlements into local languages, human rights seminars for community representatives, and legal assistance to obtain the release of minors from military service. Where the United Nations or a regional organization is present, for example, in a negotiated peace settlement, combatting underage recruitment should be included specifically in its human rights mandate, together with the provision of institutional support to local NGOs initiatives. Negative media publicity can also be used to break forced recruitment practices by armed groups, even if the first reaction may be on a self-interested basis, in the hope of gaining positive publicity and legitimacy. In addition, concerned local NGOs, religious groups or community leaders with access to opposition leaders can develop public platforms based on a moral agenda reflecting local values, custom and practice. International donors should strengthen such local initiatives, which will be most effective wherever the armed group relies heavily on the local civilian population. Foreign aid donors and international agencies should assume eighteen as the preferred age of recruitment by State and non-State entities when formulating recommendations or policy statements. A declaration of minimum standards which included a prohibition on the participation of youth under eighteen could be used by international donors to insist on compliance as a condition of aid.

Interventions to minimize *voluntary participation* can tackle the issue indirectly, by targeting structural problems, and more directly, by attempting to change perceptions of the value of participation held by youth and those around them. Throughout the field research for this study, dealing with the root causes has been the only method consistently suggested for reducing youth volunteerism, even though no particular programme or policy has ever appeared to link the two concerns explicitly. Local people and organizations may be at risk if they address such issues, but international donor governments, financial lending institutions, and international aid agencies are better placed to promote structural reform by conditioning aid on government respect for fundamental human rights. International donor pressure can inform international public opinion on the relationship between the participation of children and the root causes of the conflict.

Interventions aimed at how children appraise the decision to participate in a conflict include strengthening those who can influence a child's perception of the value of participation, such as the extended family and the community, and even combatting the myth of the warring culture and the propaganda value of child soldiers. Alternative activities, such as educational opportunities will also need to be found, in an approach that will ideally deal with the macro issues as they impact at the personal level. Improvements in socio-economic conditions are likely to be an incentive to demobilization, while family tracing, care for the homeless or orphaned, and physical and psychosocial rehabilitation can also facilitate the process. Assistance to families or communities will likely ease the burdens of reintegrating ex-combatants, and training and education for child combatants and adults who have passed their childhood years as combatants could serve as links between demobilization and local development initiatives.

Conditions and Consequences

When children's realities are defined by war's causes and by-products—displacement, separation, loss of parents, lack of food and shelter—should we not be ready for the choice that some will make? Time and again, we found young people who saw their own personal security as greater inside armed opposition movements than outside, with the other orphans, street children, refugees and displaced civilians. They found a home, stability, loyalty, discipline, empowerment, pride and respect. So long as we or their proximate communities cannot provide social support and material needs, we will have to deal with the consequences; not only the traumas of participation in conflict, but also the facts of detention or confinement as prisoners of war.

Although international law lays down no minimum standard for criminal responsibility, the general thrust of the Convention on the Rights of the Child and the juvenile justice standards endorsed by the United Nations is to recognize limited capacity. National laws and procedures do not always meet even the minimum requirements of international law, and many youth detained for reasons related to conflict go without adequate legal protection, often held for long periods without charge. The effective protection of detainees in such situations will only improve when institutions such as human rights offices or public defenders are established or strengthened, and legal aid NGOs can take up such cases without fear of reprisal. In the meantime, national juvenile justice procedures call for further investigation at the international level, for example, within the process offered by treaty monitoring bodies.

In addition to detention, other consequences for children involved in armed conflict include physical and psychological damage. Under the Convention on the Rights of the Child, every child is entitled to receive such 'protection and care as is necessary for his or her well-being'. States are obliged to 'ensure to the maximum extent possible the survival and development of the child'; to protect children from all forms of mental violence or abuse; and to strive to ensure that victims of armed conflict have access to rehabilitative care.

No systematic study appears to have been conducted into the relationship between the way children cope with exposure to violence and future choices. Some evidence suggests a connection between exposure to chronic fear as children and susceptibility to later recruitment into terrorist or armed groups, and further research here could help in developing interventions to avert youth participation at an earlier stage.

The recuperative powers of children who themselves have perpetrated violence appear greatly diminished. The fear of rejection or the danger of physical or legal retribution for acts committed during conflict can be a subjective reaction or an objective reality; together with the lack of material benefits, it may act as a deterrent to demobilization and later re-integration. Research is inconclusive, however, as to the likelihood of moral breakdown among children who actively participate in political violence and armed conflict, although young leaders, volunteers with nothing to lose, and highly politicized youth can all suffer the negative consequences of participation.

Numerous reports cite discipline problems among young former combatants and participants in civil strife, who also suffer frequent traumatic experience, PTSD (post-traumatic stress disorder), nightmares, sleep disorders and avoidance.

Just as the root causes of a conflict offer a starting point for understanding the traumatic experiences that influence some children to join armed groups, the larger processes by which a conflict is resolved are also relevant to understanding how child soldiers will come to grips with their personal war experiences. In the case of a negotiated solution involving compromises on all sides, such as amnesties, children who participated out of revenge might feel betrayed or frustrated. Again, further research is needed on the reintegration into civil society of youth whose reasons for taking up arms may or may not be addressed in the resolution of the conflict.

Responding to Recruitment and Participation

While prevention is the principal objective, we do not live in an ideal world; our recommendations on the *protection* of child soldiers must therefore be sufficiently flexible and extensive also to deal with the consequences, and to suggest an appropriate division and sharing of responsibility. Who should intervene, when and how, are questions that cannot be answered once and for all. The lack of international standing of many non-governmental entities means that local and international NGOs have a major, though not exclusive, responsibility to address the needs of populations and child soldiers in zones under NGE control; and that NGEs in turn should not hinder access to the population.

Often, the first hope may be the International Committee of the Red Cross (ICRC), which generally manages to be present in most situations of conflict. Gaining access to and protecting the victims is not necessarily automatic, however; it often depends on the ICRC maintaining a relatively low profile and refraining from going public on complaints. These limitations mean that complementary mandates must come into play, among United Nations agencies, human rights organizations, local and international NGOs.

NGOs, for example, have proven productive and effective in keeping track of those detained, establishing lines of communication to families, providing legal advice, exposing unsatisfactory detention conditions and documenting injustices. UN agencies and representatives need further encouragement to investigate and publicise the plight of child soldiers as an integral part of larger, on-going human rights investigations, for example, on disappearances, torture, detention conditions, or the security of refugee camps.

The Need for Further Research

Effective interventions to deal with the psychosocial impact of war on children are needed, based on local assessments of options and possibilities, identification of those most likely to suffer crippling consequences or to benefit from constructive outcomes. In addition, culturally appropriate responses must be developed. Research in these areas is often disdained, but in practice it has yielded informative data and innovative programmes. Even though participants may have faced the same traumatic experiences as victims generally, a portion of research and programme resources should be devoted to the former group of youngsters, and to the still larger numbers of adults who spent their entire childhoods as active combatants.

Those working with child soldiers and former participants require sound assessment tools, easily adapted to local circumstances. International agencies and NGOs could train the trainers, or prepare local child-care specialists to adapt measures, collect and analyze data, and use their results in programme development. Where there is conflict, so there will often be large numbers of traumatized children and child soldiers, in itself advance notice of the need for projects for training health and education personnel in war trauma counselling. It would be helpful to have studies of identity formation among child combatants and the problems adjusting later to a civilian identity. A review of existing practices suggests several guidelines to successful programme development and execution. Existing support structures must be reinforced, including mothers or other adult caregivers such as grandparents and teachers, who can help to dissuade children from joining an armed group. Intervention strategies should incorporate traditional practices, values and beliefs, wherever possible. Deinstitutionalization of treatment is preferred, meaning emphasis on the former combatant as a member of a larger community, and community-based strategies that reduce the stigma attached to psychological therapy. Researchers need to evaluate seriously the effectiveness of existing programme models, and whether they might be replicated in other contexts.

At the more general level, a study of the factors on which to base predictions of successful reconciliation, such as culture, resolution of the root causes of the conflict, popular perceptions of the conflict resolution process, and the material outcome of the conflict, might help international politicians and local groups structure a durable peace.

The causes and consequences of each conflict must be examined separately, in seeking a balance between the implications of an amnesty and the goals of conflict resolution, national reconciliation and rehabilitation. Forgiveness and reconciliation can be promoted by amnesties at national level, but must generally be accompanied by complementary policies. Recent experience, for example, confirms that the successful disarming of combatants needs more than just an amnesty, which alone can have negative consequences, for example, by granting impunity to known human rights violators. Abuses of the rights of children in armed conflict should be strictly monitored and reported. Abuses perpetrated *by* child soldiers may require rehabilitative responses, rather than retributive measures. Public acknowledgement of and accountability for human rights violations are important steps towards national reconciliation, and are candidates for monitoring by international and regional organizations and NGOs.

Law and Process

All areas of the law would benefit from upgrading. A significant part of international human rights law is based on the protection of children and young persons up to the age of 18, a general principle which should be central to the interpretation of Additional Protocols I and II and the Convention on the Rights of the Child. So far as recruitment is concerned, however, universal and formal acceptance of 18 as the minimum age is a key objective. International humanitarian law provides the basis for such a rule, but it needs updating and clarifying. This could be promoted from the grass roots, through national Red Cross and Red Crescent Societies, with the endorsement of the Council of Delegates and the 26th International Conference of the Red Cross and Red Crescent. It must be driven, too, by non-governmental organizations of all persuasions, using the resources of government, parliament, regional and international organizations, the media and public support.

Specific goals should include: National legislation and practice in accordance with the minimum 18 age rule; formal endorsement of the rule by the ICRC; unilateral declarations by States parties to the Convention the Rights of the Child, and eventually the development of a protocol codifying the rule; the activation or improvement of existing human rights jurisdictions.

Children in internal strife, the most common situation of conflict today, suffer because of the perceived inapplicability of international humanitarian law. Every support should be given, therefore, to efforts to raise the standards, for example through Declarations of Minimum Humanitarian Standards, provided they include the minimum age 18 rule and clarify the responsibilities of adults as recruiters or commanders. Such an initiative also could be supported by national Red Cross and Red Crescent Societies.

The principles of the United Nations, binding upon the Organization, include promoting 'universal respect for, and observance of, human rights and fundamental freedoms for all without distinction as to race, sex, language, or religion.' The UN human rights machinery, slow as it is, must be understood in the light of this overall policy goal. For example, bringing complaints to the notice of the Commission on Human Rights, helps it to identify situations involving 'a consistent pattern of gross and reliably attested violations'. NGOs play an important role as sources of information and also in bringing such issues before the Sub-Commission on the Protection of Minorities and the Prevention of Discrimination so that patterns of human rights violations can be brought to the attention of the Commission itself. Both these processes in turn feed into the General Assembly.

UNHCR has expressly recognized its responsibilities towards children in refugee camps, who must be protected from recruitment by governments and non-governmental entities alike. The High Commissioner's reports are one way in which the problems of refugee children can be brought to the attention of a wider forum. UNHCR's strength as a human rights organization lies in the fact that it is widely represented throughout the world, particularly in areas of conflict involving both refugees and child soldiers.

UNICEF, which has a specific role under the CRC, should develop guidelines for its own officials to report on recruitment and related practices, while also encouraging local NGOs to assume monitoring and reporting responsibilities.

The ICRC, although an obvious first avenue of complaint wherever a party to a conflict appears to be acting in violation of its obligations under the Geneva Conventions and/or the Additional Protocols, often has very limited scope of action. The recently established International Fact-Finding Commission, which has offered its services in the investigation of *all* violations of humanitarian law, including those committed in civil conflict, might be supported as a possible alternative monitoring mechanism, relieving the ICRC of involvement in activities that potentially compromise its impartiality.

In addition to the 'political' human rights bodies, advocates for children should consider whether universal and regional treaty monitoring committees offer any channel for recourse, notwithstanding their particular focus and lengthy procedures.

The Committee on the Rights of the Child deserves particularly close attention, especially given the number of ratifying States and the lack of provisions for derogation from the CRC. The Committee has already announced that it will develop urgent action procedures for children, draft a general comment on child recruitment, and promote an optional protocol establishing minimum age 18. This Committee is also highly accessible to NGOs, and by international agencies having specific responsibilities towards children, such as UNICEF and UNHCR.

Politics and Pressure

Human rights and humanitarian law mechanisms have a major weakness in their inability to reach NGEs directly, and in their lack of an effective fact-finding capacity; both defects reflect traditional conceptions of sovereignty and non-intervention, but also emphasize the importance of combatting child recruitment through political bodies, to bring pressure on those responsible and, above all, to deal with the systemic or root causes that lead children to take up arms. Discussion and investigation must be promoted in international fora, which in turn should be encouraged to see certain basic human values, including the principle of non-recruitment and non-participation, as essential conditions of membership, thus bringing home the message that those seeking recognition and 'legitimacy' through armed conflict already have international responsibilities.

Under-age recruitment should be recognized as an obstacle of principle to economic assistance and to many levels of co-operation, making conditionality of aid a lever in defence of human rights. Above all, there must be increased international support for local initiatives, such as legal advice and protection processes and the implementation of programmes of response. Non-governmental assistance can be especially fruitful in marshalling a broad, cross-regional approach to practices in a particular country, or in covering the full spectrum of human rights monitoring and investigating institutions.

Knowledge, Dissemination and Access

Knowing about rights, standards and procedures is often the first step to protection. The broadest dissemination of international rules is therefore essential, but rules must be understood, assimilated, and respected over time. Here, National Red Cross and Red Crescent Societies, indigenous non-governmental organizations, other NGOs, and the media have particular responsibilities to spread the word.

Certain rules are straightforward: No child under 15 shall be recruited into the armed forces. This 'binds' States whether they have ratified the Geneva Conventions, the Additional Protocols, and the Convention on the Right of the Child, or not; for it is a rule of customary international law. The further principle that no child or youth up to the age of 18 shall be recruited or allowed to participate in conflict is also simply stated; even if its roots are a little less deep, it is supported by the general principles of international humanitarian law, and by the fundamental rules that govern the protection of the child.

Local and international non-governmental organizations should co-operate to develop the practical tools for accessing available protection systems, and for sensitizing the media and the public to the needs of children in war. A measure of regionalization and internationalization will ensure a high profile for those who violate the rights of children, and that appropriate political, legal and material pressure is brought to bear in every quarter.

Together with knowledge and understanding goes credible and trustworthy evidence. Human rights monitors the world over need to collect accounts of events, ensure the reliability of sources and information, and if possible provide corroboration or data to show consistent patterns of behaviour on the part of governments or non-government entities. Monitoring and reporting are areas in which co-operation among non-governmental organizations can compensate both for lack of resources, and for the daunting breadth of human rights concerns. A strong case can be made for developing a database on the recruitment, conscription and participation of children and youth in armed conflict, to be managed and maintained by an independent non-governmental organization, operating within and subject to a wider international network. Information relating to child soldiers, such as reports on the practice of governments and non-government entities, could be shared on a network basis, thereby encouraging the development of cross-regional and cross-institutional strategies; and treated and stored for access and analysis by all concerned, either electronically or through a regular document dissemination or exchange facility. The advantages of centralizing information, understood in a non-exclusive and non-monopolistic sense, include the concentration of resources that can be brought to bear upon the data, and the real possibility of assisting local initiatives, such as legal challenges or submissions to regional, political and supervisory institutions. A strong information base can also contribute effectively to the promotional aspects of the struggle on behalf of children involved in conflict, for example, by providing a credible resource for the media.

Annex

Ratification of the Convention on the Rights of the Child

—

International Humanitarian Law and Human Rights Instruments

—

Voting Age and Military Age by Country

The following sources have been used in the compilation of this table:

Blaustein, A. and Gisbert, F., eds., *Constitutions of the World*, Oceania, New York, 1992

Keegan, J., ed., *World Armies*, Gale Research, 1993

Kopley, G., ed., *Defense and Foreign Affairs Handbook*, Media Corp., Virginia, 1990-91

Kurian, G.T., *Encyclopedia of the Third World*, Facts on File, 4th ed., New York, 1992

Thomas, A. and Riley, E., *World Elections*, Facts on File, New York, 1985

Inter-Parliamentary Union, *Electoral Systems: A World-Wide Comparative Survey*, Geneva, 1993

United Nations, 'Conscientious Objection to Military Service,' Report prepared by the Sub-Commission on Prevention of Discrimination and Protection of Minorities: UN doc. E/CN.4/Sub.2/1983/30

United Nations, 'Contemporary Forms of Slavery: the Adoption of Children for Commercial Purposes and the Enrolment of Children in Governmental and Non-governmental Armed Forces,' Report of the Secretary-General: UN doc. E/CN.4/Sub.2/1990/43

United Nations, 'Contemporary Forms of Slavery: the Enrolment of Children in Governmental and Non-governmental Armed Forces,' Report of the Secretary-General: UN doc. E/CN.4/Sub.2/1992/35

Many National Red Cross and Red Crescent Societies, and the delegates and legal officers of the International Committee of the Red Cross, provided detailed replies, including texts or extracts from relevant nationals laws and regulations, to a questionnaire distributed throughout the International Red Cross and Red Crescent Movement. The proceedings of the recently established UN Committee on the Rights of the Child were also monitored, as were the country reports so far submitted to the Committee. Sources of national legislation and practice are not cited for reasons of space, but the documentation can be consulted in the library of the Henry Dunant Institute.

The table uses the following abbreviations:

GC1949	The First, Second, Third and Fourth Geneva Conventions of 12 August 1949
GC1,II,III1949	The First, Second and Third Geneva Conventions of 12 August 1949
API	Additional Protocol I of 8 June 1977 to the 1949 Geneva Conventions
APII	Additional Protocol II of 8 June 1977 to the 1949 Geneva Conventions
ECHR1950	European Convention on Human Rights, 1950
ACHR1969	American Convention on Human Rights, 1969 (Pact of San José)
ACHPR1981	African Charter on Human and Peoples' Rights, 1981 (Banjul Charter)
ICCPR1966	International Covenant on Civil and Political Rights, 1966
ICESCR1966	International Covenant on Economic, Social and Cultural Rights, 1966

Notes:

The information provided is correct to 30 November 1993. A date in brackets indicates that the State has signed but not yet ratified the Convention on the Rights of the Child. In the column, Military Age, (C) indicates the age for compulsory and (V) the age for voluntary service.

Country	Convention on the Rights of the Child	Humanitarian Law & Human Rights Treaties	Voting Age	Military Age (C) & (V)	Conscription ?
Afghanistan	(27/9/1990)	GC1949 ICCPR1966 ICESR1966		15(C)	Yes
Albania	27/2/1992	GC1949 API APII ICCPR1966 ICESR1966	18	18(C)	Yes
Algeria	16/4/1993	GC1949 API APII ICCPR1966 ICESR1966 ACHPR1981		19(C)	Yes
Andorra		GC1949			
Angola	5/12/1990	GC1949 API	18	18(C)	Yes
Antigua & Barbuda	5/10/1993	GC1949 API APII	18		
Argentina[1]	4/12/1990	GC1949 API APII ICCPR1966 ICESR1966 ACHR1969	18	19(C)	Yes
Armenia	23/6/1993	GC1949 API APII			
Australia	17/12/1990	GC1949 API APII ICCPR1966 ICESR1966	18	18(C) 17(V)	No

1   Argentina stated on ratification of the CRC that the use of children in armed conflict should have been formally forbidden in the Convention, and that the definition of children should be understood as meaning every human being from conception till 18 years old.

Country	Convention on the Rights of the Child	Humanitarian Law & Human Rights Treaties	Voting Age	Military Age (C) & (V)	Conscription?
Austria	6/8/1992	GC1949 API APII ICCPR1966 ICESR1966 ECHR1950	19	18(C) 17(V)	Yes
Azerbaijan	13/8/1992	GC1949 API APII ICCPR1966 ICESCR1966			
Bahamas	20/2/1991	GC1949 API APII	18		No
Bahrain	13/2/1992	GC1949 API APII		18(V)	No
Bangladesh	3/8/1990	GC1949 API APII	18	17(V)	No
Barbados	9/10/1990	GC1949 API APII ICCPR1966 ICESR1966 ACHR1969	18		No
Belarus	1/10/1990	GC1949 API APII ICCPR1966 ICESR1966	18		Yes

Country	Convention on the Rights of the Child	Humanitarian Law & Human Rights Treaties	Voting Age	Military Age (C) & (V)	Conscription?
Belgium	16/12/1991	GC1949 API APII ICCPR1966 ICESR1966 ECHR1950	18	18(C) 17(V)	Yes[2]
Belize	2/5/1990	GC1949 API APII ICCPR1966 ICESR1966	18		No
Benin	3/8/1990	GC1949 API APII ACHPR1981	18		Yes
Bhutan	1/8/1990	GC1949	18	18(V)	No
Bolivia	26/6/1990	GC1949 API APII ICCPR1966 ICESR1966 ACHR1969	21	21(C)	Yes
Bosnia & Herzegovina	1/9/1993	GC1949 API APII			
Botswana		GC1949 API APII ACHPR1981	21		No
Brazil	24/9/1990	GC1949 API APII	16	19(C)	Yes
Brunei Darussalam		GC1949 API APII			No

2   Compulsory military service is to be abolished with effect from 1 Jan. 1994.

Country	Convention on the Rights of the Child	Humanitarian Law & Human Rights Treaties	Voting Age	Military Age (C) & (V)	Conscription ?
Bulgaria	3/6/1991	GC1949 API APII ICCPR1966 ICESR1966	18	18(C)	Yes
Burkina Faso	31/8/1991	GC1949 API APII ACHPR1981	18		Yes
Burundi	19/10/1990	GC1949 API APII ICCPR1966 ICESR1966 ACHPR1981			No
Cambodia	15/10/1992	GC1949			
Cameroon	11/1/1993	GC1949 API APII ICCPR1966 ICESR1966 ACHPR1981	20		No
Canada	13/12/1991	GC1949 API APII ICCPR1966 ICESCR1966 ACHR1969	18	18(V)	No
Cape Verde	4/6/1992	GC1949 ACHPR1981	18		Yes
Central African Republic	23/4/1992	GC1949 API APII ICCPR1966 ICESCR1966 ACHPR1981	18		No

Country	Convention on the Rights of the Child	Humanitarian Law & Human Rights Treaties	Voting Age	Military Age (C) & (V)	Conscription ?
Chad	2/10/1990	GC1949 ACHPR1981			No
Chile	13/8/1990	GC1949 API APII ICCPR1966 ICESCR1966 ACHR1969	18	18(C) 16(V)	Yes
China	2/3/1992	GC1949 API APII	18	18(C)	Yes
Colombia[3]	28/1/1991	GC1949 API ICCPR1966 ICESCR1966 ACHR1969	18	18(C)	Yes
Comoros	22/6/1993	GC1949 API APII ACHPR1981	18		
Congo	14/10/1993	GC1949 API APII ICCPR1966 ICESCR1966 ACHPR1981	18	20(C) 18(V)	No
Costa Rica	21/8/1990	GC1949 API APII ICCPR1966 ICESCR1966 ACHR1969	18	18[4]	No
Côte d'Ivoire	4/2/1991	GC1949 API APII	21	21(C)	Yes

3 Colombia stated on ratification that the minimum age of conscription should be 18 years.
4 In the event that military forces are established.

Country	Convention on the Rights of the Child	Humanitarian Law & Human Rights Treaties	Voting Age	Military Age (C) & (V)	Conscription ?
Croatia	12/10/1992	GC1949 API APII ICCPR1966 ICESCR1966	18	18(C)	Yes
Cuba	21/8/1991	GC1949 API	16		Yes
Cyprus	7/2/1991	GC1949 API ICCPR1966 ICESCR1966 ECHR1950	21	18(C)	Yes
Czech Republic	22/2/1993	GC1949 API APII ICCPR1966 ICESCR1966 ECHR1950	18	18(C)	Yes
Democratic People's Republic of Korea	21/9/1990	GC1949 API ICCPR1966 ICESCR1966	17		Yes
Denmark	19/7/1991	GC1949 API APII ICCPR1966 ICESCR1966 ECHR1950	18	18(C)	No
Djibouti	6/12/1990	GC1949 API APII	18		
Dominica	13/3/1991	GC1949	18		
Dominican Republic	11/6/1991	GC1949 ICCPR1966 ICESCR1966 ACHR1969	18	18(C)	Yes

Country	Convention on the Rights of the Child	Humanitarian Law & Human Rights Treaties	Voting Age	Military Age (C) & (V)	Conscription ?
Ecuador	23/3/1990	GC1949 API APII ICCPR1966 ICESCR1966 ACHR1969	18	19(C) 18(V)	Yes
Egypt	6/7/1990	GC1949 ICCPR1966 ICESCR1966 ACHPR1981	18	18(C)	Yes
El Salvador	10/7/1990	GC1949 API APII ICCPR1966 ICESCR1966 ACHR1969	18	18(C) 16(V)	Yes
Equatorial Guinea	15/6/1992	GC1949 API APII ICCPR1966 ICESCR1966 ACHPR1981	18	18(C)	Yes
Estonia	21/10/1991	GC1949 API APII ICCPR1966 ICESCR1966 ECHR1950	18	18(C)	
Ethiopia	14/5/1991	GC1949		18(C)	Yes
Fiji	13/8/1993	GC1949	21		No
Finland	20/6/1991	GC1949 API APII ICCPR1966 ICESCR1966 ECHR1950	18	18(C) 17(V)	Yes

Country	Convention on the Rights of the Child	Humanitarian Law & Human Rights Treaties	Voting Age	Military Age (C) & (V)	Conscription ?
France	7/8/1990	GC1949 APII ICCPR1966 ICESCR1966 ECHR1950	18	18(C)	Yes
Gabon	(26/1/1990)	GC1949 API APII ICCPR1966 ICESCR1966 ACHPR1981	21		No
Gambia	8/8/1990	GC1949 API APII ICCPR1966 ICESCR1966 ACHPR1981	21		No
Georgia		GC1949 API APII	18		
Germany	6/3/1992	GC1949 API APII ICCPR1966 ICESCR1966 ECHR1950	18	18(C) 17(V)	Yes
Ghana	5/2/1990	GC1949 API APII ACHPR1981			No
Greece	13/5/1993	GC1949 API APII ICESCR1966 ECHR1950	18	18(C) 16(V)	Yes

Country	Convention on the Rights of the Child	Humanitarian Law & Human Rights Treaties	Voting Age	Military Age (C) & (V)	Conscription ?
Grenada	5/11/1990	GC1949 ICCPR1966 ICESCR1966 ACHR1969	18		No
Guatemala	6/6/1990	GC1949 API APII ICESCR1966 ACHR1969	18	18(C) 15(V)	Yes[5]
Guinea	13/7/1990	GC1949 API APII ICCPR1966 ICESCR1966 ACHPR1981		19(V)	No
Guinea-Bissau	20/8/1990	GC1949 API APII ACHPR1981			
Guyana	14/1/1991	GC1949 API APII ICCPR1966 ICESCR1966	18		No
Haiti	(26/1/1990)	GC1949 ICCPR1966 ACHR1969	21		Yes
Holy See	20/4/1990	GC1949 API APII			No
Honduras	10/8/1990	GC1949 ICESCR1966 ACHR1969	18	18(C) 17(V)	Yes

5　Fifteen year-olds may be required to volunteer to serve in Civil Defence Patrols.

Country	Convention on the Rights of the Child	Humanitarian Law & Human Rights Treaties	Voting Age	Military Age (C) & (V)	Conscription ?
Hungary	7/10/1991	GC1949 API APII ICCPR1966 ICESCR1966 ECHR1950	18	18(C)	Yes
Iceland	28/10/1992	GC1949 API APII ICCPR1966 ICESCR1966 ECHR1950	18	N/a[6]	
India	11/12/1992	GC1949 ICCPR1966 ICESCR1966	18		No
Indonesia	5/9/1990	GC1949	17	17	No
Iran	(5/9/1991)	GC1949 ICCPR1966 ICESCR1966	16	(C) (V) No age limits	Yes
Iraq		GC1949 ICCPR1966 ICESCR1966	18	19(C) 18(V)	Yes
Ireland	28/9/1992	GC1949 ICCPR1966 ICESCR1966 ECHR1950	18	18(V)	No
Israel	3/10/1991	GC1949 ICCPR1966 ICESCR1966	18	18(C) 17(V)	Yes
Italy	5/9/1991	GC1949 API APII ICCPR1966 ICESCR1966 ECHR1950	18	18(C)	Yes

6   No armed forces.

Country	Convention on the Rights of the Child	Humanitarian Law & Human Rights Treaties	Voting Age	Military Age (C) & (V)	Conscription ?
Jamaica	14/5/1991	GC1949 API APII ICCPR1966 ICESCR1966 ACHR1969	18		No
Japan	(21/9/1990)	GC1949 ICCPR1966 ICESCR1966	20	18(V)	No
Jordan	24/5/1991	GC1949 API APII ICCPR1966 ICESCR1966	19	18(C)	Yes
Kazakhstan		GC1949 API APII			
Kenya	30/7/1990	GC1949 ICCPR1966 ICESCR1966	18		No
Kiribati		GC1949	18		No
Kuwait	21/10/1991	GC1949 API APII	21	18(C) 18(V)	Yes
Kyrgyzstan		GC1949 API APII			
Laos	8/5/1991	GC1949 API APII	18	15(C)	Yes
Latvia	14/4/1992	GC1949 API APII ICCPR1966 ICESR1966	18		

Country	Convention on the Rights of the Child	Humanitarian Law & Human Rights Treaties	Voting Age	Military Age (C) & (V)	Conscription ?
Lebanon	14/5/1991	GC1949 ICCPR1966 ICESCR1966	21		No
Lesotho	10/3/1992	GC1949 ACHPR1981		18(V)	No
Liberia	4/6/1993	GC1949 API APII ACHPR1981			
Libyan Arab Jamahiriya	15/4/1993	GC1949 API APII ICCPR1966 ICESCR1966 ACHPR1981		18(C) 14(V)	Yes
Liechtenstein	(30/9/1990)	GC1949 API APII ECHR1950	20	N/a[7]	No
Lithuania	31/1/1992	GC1,II,III1949 ICCPR1966	18	19(C)	Yes
Luxembourg	(21/3/1990)	GC1949 API APII ICCPR1966 ICESCR1966 ECHR1950	18	17(V)	No
Macedonia	26/10/1993	GC1949 API APII			
Madagascar	19/3/1991	GC1949 API APII ICCPR1966 ICESCR1966			Yes

7   Armed forces abolished in 1868.

Country	Convention on the Rights of the Child	Humanitarian Law & Human Rights Treaties	Voting Age	Military Age (C) & (V)	Conscription ?
Malawi	2/1/1991	GC1949 API APII ACHPR1981	21	18(V)	No
Malaysia		GC1949	21		No
Maldives	11/2/1991	GC1949 API APII	21		No
Mali	20/9/1990	GC1949 API APII ICCPR1966 ICESCR1966 ACHPR1981	18		Yes
Malta	30/9/1990	GC1949 API APII ICCPR1966 ECHR1950	18		No
Marshall Islands	4/10/1993				
Mauritania	16/5/1991	GC1949 API APII ACHPR1981	18	16(V)	No
Mauritius	26/7/1990	GC1949 API APII ICCPR1966 ICESCR1966	18		No
Mexico	21/9/1990	GC1949 API ICCPR1966 ICESCR1966 ACHR1969	18	17(C)	Yes

Country	Convention on the Rights of the Child	Humanitarian Law & Human Rights Treaties	Voting Age	Military Age (C) & (V)	Conscription ?
Micronesia, Federated States of	5/5/1993				
Moldova	26/1/1993	GC1949 API APII	18		
Monaco	21/6/1993	GC1949	21	19(V)	No
Mongolia	5/7/1990	GC1949 ICCPR1966 ICESCR1966	18	18(C)	Yes
Morocco	21/6/1993	GC1949 ICCPR1966 ICESCR1966	20	18(C)	Yes
Mozambique	(30/9/1990)	GC1949 API ACHPR1981	18	18(C)	Yes
Myanmar	15/7/1991	GC1949	18	18(V)	No
Namibia	30/9/1990	GC1949	18	16(C)	Yes
Nauru			20		No
Nepal	14/9/1990	GC1949 ICCPR1966 ICESCR1966	18	18(V)	No
Netherlands	(26/1/1990)	GC1949 API APII ICCPR1966 ICESCR1966 ECHR1950	18	19(C) 17(V)	Yes
New Zealand	6/4/1993	GC1949 API APII ICCPR1966 ICESCR1966	18	16(V)[8]	No

8   Volunteers may join under 18 with parental consent, or if married. Age limits for liability to 'active service overseas' are 18 (army and air force) and $16\frac{1}{2}$ (navy).

Country	Convention on the Rights of the Child	Humanitarian Law & Human Rights Treaties	Voting Age	Military Age (C) & (V)	Conscription ?
Nicaragua	5/10/1990	GC1949 ICCPR1966 ICESCR1966 ACHR1969	16	17(C)	Yes
Niger	30/9/1990	GC1949 API APII ICCPR1966 ICESCR1966 ACHPR1981			Yes
Nigeria	19/4/1991	GC1949 API APII ACHPR1981	18	18(V)	No
Norway	8/1/1991	GC1949 API APII ICCPR1966 ICESCR1966 ECHR1950	18	18(C) 17(V)	Yes
Oman		GC1949 API APII			No
Pakistan	12/11/1990	GC1949	21	18(V)	No
Panama	12/12/1990	GC1949 ICCPR1966 ICESCR1966 ACHR1969	18		No
Papua New Guinea	2/3/1993	GC1949	18		No
Paraguay	25/9/1990	GC1949 API APII ACHR1969	18		Yes

Country	Convention on the Rights of the Child	Humanitarian Law & Human Rights Treaties	Voting Age	Military Age (C) & (V)	Conscription?
Peru	4/9/1990	GC1949 API APII ICCPR1966 ICESCR1966 ACHR1969			Yes
Philippines	21/8/1990	GC1949 APII ICCPR1966 ICESCR1966	18	18(C)	Yes
Poland	7/6/1991	GC1949 API APII ICCPR1966 ICESCR1966 ECHR1950	18	18(C) 17(V)	Yes
Portugal	21/9/1990	GC1949 API APII ICCPR1966 ICESCR1966 ECHR1950	18	21(C)	Yes
Qatar		GC1949 API			No
Republic of Korea	20/11/1991	GC1949 API APII ICCPR1966 ICESCR1966	20	18(C)	Yes
Romania	28/9/1990	GC1949 API APII ICCPR1966 ICESCR1966	18	18(C)	Yes

Country	Convention on the Rights of the Child	Humanitarian Law & Human Rights Treaties	Voting Age	Military Age (C) & (V)	Conscription ?
Russian Federation	16/8/1990	GC1949￼API￼APII￼ICCPR1966￼ICESCR1966	18	18(C)	Yes
Rwanda	24/1/1991	GC1949￼API￼APII￼ICCPR1966￼ICESCR1966￼ACHPR1981	18	18(V)	No
Saint Kitts & Nevis	24/7/1990	GC1949￼API￼APII	18		No
Saint Lucia	16/6/1993	GC1949￼API￼APII	18		No
Saint Vincent & the Grenadines	26/10/1993	GC1949￼API￼APII￼ICCPR1966￼ICESCR1966	18		No
Samoa	(30/9/1990)	GC1949￼API￼APII	21		No
San Marino	25/11/1991	GC1949￼ICCPR1966￼ICESCR1966￼ECHR1950	18	18(C)	Yes
Sao Tome & Principe	14/5/1991	GC1949￼ACHPR1981	18		
Saudi Arabia		GC1949￼API			Yes

Country	Convention on the Rights of the Child	Humanitarian Law & Human Rights Treaties	Voting Age	Military Age (C) & (V)	Conscription ?
Senegal	30/7/1990	GC1949 API APII ICCPR1966 ICESCR1966 ACHPR1981	21	18(V)	No
Seychelles	7/9/1990	GC1949 API APII	18		No
Sierra Leone	18/6/1990	GC1949 API APII ACHPR1981	18		No
Singapore		GC1949	21	18(C)	Yes
Slovak Republic	28/5/1993	GC1949 API APII ICCPR1966 ICESCR1966 ECHR1950	18	18(C)	Yes
Slovenia	6/7/1992	GC1949 API APII ICCPR1966 ICESCR1966	18	18(C)	Yes
Solomon Islands		ICCPR1966 ICESCR1966	18		No
Somalia		GC1949 ICCPR1966 ICESCR1966 ACHPR1981	18		
South Africa		GC1949	18	17(C) 16(V)	Yes

Country	Convention on the Rights of the Child	Humanitarian Law & Human Rights Treaties	Voting Age	Military Age (C) & (V)	Conscription ?
Spain[9]	6/12/1990	GC1949 API APII ICCPR1966 ICESCR1966 ECHR1950	18	20(C)	Yes
Sri Lanka	12/7/1991	GC1949 ICCPR1966 ICESCR1966	18		No
Sudan	3/8/1990	GC1949 ICCPR1966 ICESCR1966 ACHPR1981		18(V)	No
Suriname	1/3/1993	GC1949 API APII ICCPR1966 ICESCR1966 ACHR1969	18		No
Swaziland	(22/8/1990)	GC1949	18	18(V)	No
Sweden	29/6/1990	GC1949 API APII ICCPR1966 ICESCR1966 ECHR1950	18	18(C)	Yes
Switzerland	(1/5/1991)	GC1949 API APII ECHR1950	20	20(C)	Yes
Syrian Arab Republic	15/7/1993	GC1949 API ICCPR1966 ICESCR1966	18	19(C)	Yes

9   Spain stated on ratifying the CRC that the age of 15 was too low for conscription.

Country	Convention on the Rights of the Child	Humanitarian Law & Human Rights Treaties	Voting Age	Military Age (C) & (V)	Conscription ?
Tajikistan	26/10/1993	GC1949 API APII			
Thailand	27/3/1992	GC1949	20		Yes
Togo	1/8/1990	GC1949 API APII ICCPR1966 ICESCR1966 ACHPR1981			No
Tonga		GC1949	21		No
Trinidad & Tobago	5/12/1991	GC1949 ICCPR1966 ICESCR1966	18		No
Tunisia	30/1/1992	GC1949 API APII ICCPR1966 ICESCR1966 ACHPR1981	20	20(C) 18(V)	Yes
Turkey	(14/9/1990)	GC1949 ECHR1950	19	20(C)	Yes
Turkmenistan	20/9/1993	GC1949 API APII			
Tuvalu		GC1949	18		No
Uganda	17/8/1990	GC1949 API APII ICESCR1966 ACHPR1981	18		No

Country	Convention on the Rights of the Child	Humanitarian Law & Human Rights Treaties	Voting Age	Military Age (C) & (V)	Conscription ?
Ukraine	28/8/1991	GC1949 API APII ICCPR1966 ICESCR1966	18	18(C)	Yes
United Arab Emirates		GC1949 API APII			No
United Kingdom	16/12/1991	GC1949 ICCPR1966 ICESCR1966 ECHR1950	18	16(V)[10]	No
United Republic of Tanzania	10/6/1991	GC1949 API APII ICCPR1966 ICESCR1966 ACHPR1981	18	18	No
United States of America		GC1949 ICCPR1966	18	18(C) 17(V)	No
Uruguay[11]	20/11/1990	GC1949 API APII ICCPR1966 ICESCR1966 ACHR1969	18	18(C) 18(V)	Yes
Uzbekistan		GC1949 API APII	18		
Vanuatu	7/7/1993	GC1949 API APII	18		No

10   Exact ages for voluntary enlistment vary, depending on service entered; those under 17 are not assigned to active service.
11   Uruguay stated on ratification of the CRC that 18 should be the minimum age for both compulsory and voluntary military service.

Country	Convention on the Rights of the Child	Humanitarian Law & Human Rights Treaties	Voting Age	Military Age (C) & (V)	Conscription ?
Venezuela	13/9/1990	GC1949 ICCPR1966 ICESCR1966 ACHR1969	18	18(C)	Yes
Vietnam	28/2/1990	GC1949 API ICCPR1966 ICESCR1966	18	18(C)	Yes
Yemen	1/5/1991	GC1949 API APII ICCPR1966 ICESCR1966			
Yugoslavia (Serbia & Montenegro)	3/1/1991	GC1949 API APII ICCPR1966 ICESCR1966	18	18(C) 17(V)	Yes
Zaire	27/9/1990	GC1949 API APII ICCPR1966 ICESCR1966 ACHPR1981	18	18(C)	Yes
Zambia	6/12/1991	GC1949 ICCPR1966 ICESCR1966 ACHPR1981	18		No
Zimbabwe	11/9/1990	GC1949 API APII ICCPR1966 ICESCR1966 ACHPR1981	18	18(V)	No

BIBLIO-

GRAPHY

Abi-Saab, G., 'Respect of Humanitarian Norms in International Conflicts', in Independent Commission on International Humanitarian Issues, *Modern Wars*, 1986, 60.

Actes de la Conférence diplomatique sur la réaffirmation et le développement du Droit international humanitaire applicable dans les Conflits Armés, Geneva (1974-1977).

Africa Watch, *Conspicuous Destruction: War, Famine and the Reform Process in Mozambique*, July 1992.

Ahlström, C., with Nordquist, K-A., *Casualties of Conflict: Report for the World Campaign for the Protection of Victims of War*, Dept. of Peace and Conflict Research, Uppsala University, 1991.

Al Haq, *Israel's War against Education in the Occupied West Bank: A Penalty for the Future*, Ramallah, Nov. 1988.

Alston, P., 'The Committee on Economic, Social and Cultural Rights,' in Alston, P., ed., *The United Nations and Human Rights*, 1992, 473.

Alston, P., 'The Commission on Human Rights,' in Alston, P., ed., *The United Nations and Human Rights*, 1992, 126.

Alston, P., ed., *The United Nations and Human Rights: A Critical Appraisal*, Clarendon Press, Oxford, 1992.

Americas Watch and Lawyers Committee for International Human Rights, *Free Fire: A Report on Human Rights in El Salvador*, Aug. 1984.

Americas Watch, *The Civilian Toll (1986-1987)*, Washington D.C., Aug. 1987.

Americas Watch, *Violation of Fair Trial Guarantees by the FMLN's Ad Hoc Courts*, Washington D.C., May 1990.

Americas Watch, *Into the Quagmire: Human Rights and U.S. Policy in Peru*, Washington D.C., Sept. 1991.

Americas Watch, *Peru: Civil Society and Democracy under Fire*, Washington D.C., Aug. 1992.

Asia Watch, *Cycles of Violence: Human Rights in Sri Lanka since the Indo-Sri Lanka Agreement*, Washington, D.C., 1987.

Asia Watch, *Human Rights in Burma (Myanmar)*, New York, May 1990.

Asia Watch, *The Philippines. Violations of the Laws of War by both Sides,* New York, Aug. 1990.

Attias, Ernesto & Cohn, Ilene, *Infancia y Guerra: Informe sobre 'El Impacto Psicosocial de la Violencia en los Niños de America Central'*, UNICEF Area Office for Central America, Mar. 1990.

B'Tselem, (Israeli Information Centre for Human Rights in the Occupied Territories), 'House Demolitions,' *Information Sheet: Update,* Jerusalem, Jun. 1989.

B'Tselem, 'Violence against Minors in Detention,' *Information Sheet: Update,* Jerusalem, June-July 1990.

B'Tselem, 'Closure of Schools and Other Setbacks to the Education System in the Occupied Territories,' *Information Sheet: Update,* Jerusalem, Sept.-Oct. 1990.

B'Tselem, 'House Demolition and Sealing as a Form of Punishment in the West Bank and Gaza Strip,' *Information Sheet: Update,* Jerusalem, Nov. 1990.

B'Tselem, 'The Activities of "Hotline: Centre for the Defense of the Individual",' *Information Sheet*, Jerusalem, Aug. 1991.

B'Tselem, *The Interrogation of Palestinians during the Intifada: Follow-up to March 1991 Report*, Jerusalem, Mar. 1992.

Bahnassi, Ahmad Fathi, 'Criminal Responsibility in Islamic Law,' in Bassiouni, M. Cherif, ed., *The Islamic Criminal Justice System*, London, 1982, 192.

Baker, Ahmad, M., 'The Psychosocial Effects of Mistreatment During Detention on Palestinian Youth,' in *Children Imprisoned*, The DataBase Project on Palestinian Human Rights, Jerusalem (1989).

Baker, Ahmad M., 'The Impact of the Intifada on the Mental Health of Palestinian Children Living in the Occupied Territories,' Paper presented to the 67th Annual Meeting of the American Orthospychiatric Association, Miami, Fla., Apr. 1990.

Bedjaoui, M., 'Humanitarian law at a time of failing national and international consensus', in Independent Commission on International Humanitarian Issues, *Modern Wars*, 1986, 1.

Boothby, Neil, 'Children and War,' 10 *Cultural Survival Quarterly*, No. 4 (1986).

Boothby, Neil, 'Without Moral Restraint: Children in the Midst of War', *Social Health Review*, Dec. 1987.

Boothby, Neil and Humphrey, John, 'Under the Gun - Children in Exile', V. Hamilton, ed., U.S. Committee for Refugees, Wash. D.C., 1988.

Boothby, Neil, 'Living in the War Zone,' in US Committee for Refugees, *World Refugee Survey - 1989 in Review*, pp. 40-1.

Boothby, Neil, 'Working in the War Zone: A Look at Psychological Theory and Practice from the Field,' *Mind & Human Interaction*, vol.2, no.2, Virginia, 1990, p. 33.

Boothby, Neil, Upton, Peter, & Sultan, Abubacar, 'Boy Soldiers of Mozambique', *Refugee Children*, Refugee Studies Programme, Oxford, Mar. 1992.

Bothe, M., Partsch, K.J. & Solf, W.A., *New Rules for Victims of Armed Conflicts: Commentary on the Two Protocols Additional to the Geneva Conventions of 1949*, Nijhoff, The Hague, 1982.

Byrnes, Andrew, 'The Committee against Torture,' in Alston, P., ed., *The United Nations and Human Rights*, 1992, 509-46.

Cassese, A., 'Respect of Humanitarian Norms in Non-International Conflicts' in Independent Commission on International Humanitarian Issues, *Modern Wars*, 1986, 86.

Center on War and the Child, *Uganda: Land of the Child Soldier, A Summary Report*, Eureka Springs, Ark., 1987.

Center on War and the Child, *The Recruitment and Use of Children in the Gulf War: A Summary Report*, Eureka Springs, Ark., 1988.

Center on War and the Child, *The Children of Mozambique's Killing Fields*, Eureka Springs, Ark., 1989.

Center on War and the Child, *Youth Under Fire: Military Conscription in El Salvador,* Eureka Springs, Ark., 1989.

Center on War and the Child, *Lebanon: Children in Armed Conflict from 1975-1989. A Summary Report.* Eureka Springs, Ark., 1990.

Children of War, Report from the Conference on Children of War, Stockholm, Sweden, 31 May — 2 June 1991, Raoul Wallenberg Institute, Report No. 10, Lund, 1991.

Cohn, Ilene, 'The Convention on the Rights of the Child: What it Means for Children in War,' 3 *Int'l J. Refugee Law* 100 (1991).

Committee on the Rights of the Child, Report on the Second Session: UN doc. CRC/C/10. 19 Oct. 1992.

Committee on the Rights of the Child, Report on the Third Session: UN doc. CRC/C/16, 2 Mar. 1993.

Defence for Children International, 'Report on a Mission to Iraq: Evaluation of Educational Assistance Possibilities to Iranian Child-Soldiers in Prisoner-of-War Camps in Iraq (9-15 Dec. 1983),' Geneva, 1984.

Defence for Children International, 'Report on Second Mission to Iraq (25-29 May 1984)', Geneva, 1984.

Degregori, Carlos Ivan & Belaunde, Javier de, 'Opinion', *Area Chica*, Rädda Barnen, Aug. 1992.

Dodge, Cole P., 'Child Soldiers of Uganda: What Does the Future Hold?' 10 *Cultural Survival Quarterly*, No. 4, 31, (1986).

Dodge, Cole P. & Raundalen, Magne, *Reaching Children in War: Sudan, Uganda and Mozambique*, Sigma Forlag, Norway, 1991.

Dutli, María Teresa, 'Captured Child Combatants,' *International Review of the Red Cross*, Sept-Oct 1990, 421.

Eide, A., 'The Sub-Commission on Prevention of Discrimination and Protection of Minorities,' in Alston, P., ed., *The United Nations and Human Rights*, 1992, 211.

El-Sarraj, Eyad, 'The Psycho-political state of the Palestinians before and after the Intifada', unpublished paper delivered at the Truman Institute for Peace, The Hebrew University, 20 Mar. 1988, pp.8-9.

Freeman, M. & Veerman, P., *The Ideologies of Children's Rights*, Nijhoff, Dordrecht, 1992.

Garbarino, J., 'A Note on Children and Youth in Dangerous Environments: The Palestinian Situation as a Case Study.' Erikson Institute, Chicago (undated).

Gasser, Hans-Peter, 'Scrutiny,' 9 *Aust. YB Int'l Law* 345 (1985).

Gasser, Hans-Peter, 'A Measure of Humanity in Internal Disturbances and Tensions: Proposal for a Code of Conduct,' *International Review of the Red Cross*, Jan-Feb. 1988, 38.

Goodwin-Gill, Guy S., *The Refugee in International Law*, Clarendon Press, Oxford, 1983.

Greenbaum, Charles, 'Police Violence Against Minors - Psychological Aspects,' in *Violence against Minors in Detention,* B'Tselem Information Sheet: Update June-July 1990.

Helsinki Watch/Asia Watch, *To Win the Children: Afghanistan's Other War*, (1986).

Henriquez, José Luis y Mendez, Milagros, 'Los Efectos Psicosociales de la Guerra en Niños de El Salvador', *Revista de Psicologia de El Salvador*, vol.XI, no.44, (1992), 89, UCA, San Salvador.

Hilsum, Lindsey, 'Not too small to kill', *Children First*, UNICEF/UK, Autumn 1986, pp. 16-18.

Independent Commission on International Humanitarian Issues and Rädda Barnen, *Protection of Children*. Report of the International Symposium on the Protection of Children, Amman, Jordan. Geneva. 1984.

Independent Commission on International Humanitarian Issues, *Modern Wars*, 1986, 86.

Institute for Human Rights, 1990 Declaration of Minimum Humanitarian Standards, Åbo Akademi University, Turku/Åbo, Finland, 1991.

Inter-Parliamentary Union, *Electoral Systems: A World-Wide Comparative Study*, Geneva, 1993.

International Human Rights Law Group, *The Law Group Docket*, Washington, D.C., vol.7, no.2, Dec. 1992.

International Labour Organisation, 10 *Conditions of Work Digest*, Geneva, 1991.

International Committee of the Red Cross, *The Work of the ICRC for the Benefit of Civilian Detainees in German Concentration Camps between 1939 and 1945*, (1975).

International Committee of the Red Cross, 'Action by the International Committee of the Red Cross in the Event of Breaches of International Humanitarian Law,' *International Review of the Red Cross*, Mar.-Apr. 1981, 1.

International Committee of the Red Cross, *ICRC and Children in Situation of Armed Conflict*, Geneva, 1987.

International Committee of the Red Cross, 'ICRC Protection and Assistance Activities in Situations not covered by International Humanitarian Law,' *International Review of the Red Cross*, Jan.-Feb. 1988, 9.

International Committee of the Red Cross, *Collection of Basic Texts relating to the Dissemination of International Humanitarian Law*, Geneva.

Jäckli, R., 'What does the Future hold for International Humanitarian Law?' 9 *Aust. Y.B.Int'l. Law* 384 (1985).

Johnsson, Anders B., 'Refugee Children Today,' Statement at Media Seminar on the Convention on the Rights of the Child organized by the United Nations Centre for Human Rights and the United Nations Children's Fund (UNICEF), New York, 16 Nov. 1989.

Krill, Françoise, 'The Protection of Children in Armed Conflict,' in Freeman, M. and Veerman, P., *The Ideologies of Children's Rights*, (1992), 347.

Kuttab, David, 'A Profile of the Stonethrowers', 17 *J. of Palestine Studies* 14, 18 (Spring 1988).

LAWASIA Human Rights Report, *Filipino Children in Situations of Armed Conflict*, (1989).

Leon, Rafael, 'D.L. 25564: Penalización de Menores, Absurdo sin Maquillaje', *Area Chica*, Rädda Barnen, Aug. 1992.

Louyot, Alain, *Gosses de Guerre*, Laffont, Paris, 1989.

Macksoud, Mona & Nazar, Fatima, 'The Impact of the Iraqi Occupation on the Psychosocial Development of Children in Kuwait', Kuwaiti Society for the Advancement of Arab Children, 1 Mar. 1993.

Macksoud, Mona & Aber, J. Lawrence, 'The War Experiences and Psychosocial Development of Children in Lebanon,' *Child Development,* (in press) 1993.

Marcelino, Elizabeth, 'Children at War', *Children of the Storm*, vol. 3, no.1, Children's Rehabilitation Centre, Manila, July 1991-March 1992.

Martín-Baró, Ignacio, 'La Violencia Política y la Guerra como Causas del Trauma Psicosocial en El Salvador', *Revista de Psicología de El Salvador* vol. VII, no. 28, 123-41, 1988.

Mazilu, Dimitri, Prevention of Discrimination and Protection of Children: Human Rights and Youth: UN doc. E/CN.4/Sub.2/1992/36, 18 Jun. 1992.

McGoldrick, D., *The Human Rights Committee: Its Role in the Development of the International Covenant on Civil and Political Rights*, Clarendon Press, Oxford, 1991.

Meron, Theodor, 'On the Inadequate Reach of Humanitarian and Human Rights Law and the Need for a New Instrument,' 77 *Am. J. Int'l. Law* 589 (1983).

Meron, Theodor, 'Towards a Humanitarian Declaration on Internal Strife,' 78 *Am. J. Int'l. Law* 859 (1984).

Meron, Theodor, *Human Rights in Internal Strife: Their International Protection*, Hersch Lauterpacht Memorial Lectures, Cambridge, 1987.

Meron, Theodor, 'Draft Model Declaration on Internal Strife,' *International Review of the Red Cross*, Jan-Feb. 1988, 59.

Meron, Theodor, *Human Rights and Humanitarian Norms as Customary Law*, Clarendon Press, Oxford, 1989.

Meurant, J., 'Dissemination and Education,' 9 *Aust. YB Int'l Law* 364 (1985).

Middle East Watch, 'Israeli Interrogation Methods Under Fire After Death of Detained Palestinian', *Bulletin,* Vol. 4, Issue 6, Mar. 1992.

Ministry of Justice of Israel, 'Children as Participants in the Intifada', Jerusalem, 1989.

Moumtzis, P., 'Children of War,' *Refugees*, UNHCR Quarterly Report, July 1992, pp. 30-2.

Nixon, Anne E., *The Status of Palestinian Children during the Uprising in the Occupied Territories,* 2 vols., Rädda Barnen, Jerusalem, 1990.

Opsahl, T., 'The Human Rights Committee,' in Alston, P., *The United Nations and Human Rights,* 1992, 369-443.

Palestinian Human Rights Information Centre (PHRIC), 'The Arrest, Detention and Physical Abuse of Palestinian Children', in *From the Field,* Jerusalem, Aug.-Sept. 1991.

Palestinian Human Rights Information Centre (PHRIC), *Israel's Use of Shock Torture in the Interrogation of Palestinian Detainees,* Jerusalem, 2nd ed., Jul. 1992.

Pictet, J., ed., *Commentary on the Geneva Conventions of 12 August 1949,* 4 vols., International Committee of the Red Cross, Geneva, 1952, 1956, 1958, 1959.

Plattner, Denise, 'Protection of Children in International Humanitarian Law,' *International Review of the Red Cross,* 1984, 140.

Plattner, Denise, 'La portée juridique des déclarations de respect du droit international humanitaire qui émanent de mouvements en lutte dans un conflit armé,' *Rev. belge dr. int.,* 1984-1985/1, 298.

Procurador de los Derechos Humanos, *Los Derechos Humanos: Un Compromiso por la Justicia y la Paz,* 1987-1992, Guatemala.

Procurador de Derechos Humanos, *Informe Circunstanciado de Actividades y de la Situación de los Derechos Humanos durante 1992,* Guatemala, 1993.

Quaker Office at the United Nations, *Children Bearing Military Arms,* Geneva, 1983.

Rädda Barnen, 'No Child Soldiers!' Stockholm, Sept. 1989.

Ressler, Everett M., Tortorici, Joanne M. & Marcelino, Alex, *Children in War: A Guide to the Provision of Services,* UNICEF, New York, 1993.

Robert F. Kennedy Memorial Centre for Human Rights, *Persecution by Proxy: The Civil Patrols in Guatemala,* New York, 1993.

Rosenblatt, Roger, *Children of War,* Anchor Press/Doubleday, New York, 1983.

Schindler, D. & Toman, J., *The Laws of Armed Conflict*, Sijthoff & Noordhoff, The Netherlands; Henry Dunant Institute, Geneva, 1981.

Secretariat of the Commissioner General of Rehabilitation, *A Brief on Rehabilitation of Youth in Sri Lanka*, Ministry of Youth Affairs & Sports, Colombo, (undated).

Singer, Sandra, 'The Protection of Children during Armed Conflict Situations,' *International Review of the Red Cross*, May-June 1986, 133.

Subah, Marion & Friesen, Delores, *Trauma Healing for Children*, Brochure produced for the Christian Health Association of Liberia, Monrovia (1992).

Thomson, J.F., 'Repression of Violations,' 9 *Aust. YB. Int'l Law* 325 (1985).

Torres, Maritess, 'Children in Combat,' in *Children of the Storm*, Children's Rehabilitation Centre, Philippines (1992).

UNHCR, *Note on Refugee Children*: UN doc. E/SCP/46, (9 Jul. 1987).

UNHCR, *Guidelines on Refugee Children*, Geneva, Aug. 1988.

UNHCR Executive Committee, Conclusion No. 46; Report of the 38th Session: UN doc. A/AC.96/702, 22 Oct. 1987.

UNICEF West Bank and Gaza Strip, *The Situation of Palestinian Children in the West Bank and Gaza Strip* (Draft), Jerusalem, Jul. 1992, p.96.

UNICEF Colombo, *A Profile of the Sri Lankan Child in Crisis and Conflict*, (1990).

UNICEF West Bank and Gaza Strip, *The Strategy for the 1992-1994 UNICEF Programme of Cooperation in the West Bank and Gaza Strip*, Jun. 1992.

United Nations, The Recruitment of Children into the Armed Forces: UN doc. E/CN.4/Sub.2/1990/43, 26 Jun. 1990.

United Nations, Report on a Visit to Sri Lanka by three members of the Working Group on Enforced or Involuntary Disappearances (7-18 October 1991): UN doc. E/CN.4/1992/18/Add.1 (8 Jan. 1992).

United Nations, The Recruitment of Children into Governmental Armed Forces and Non-Governmental Armed Forces: UN doc. E/CN.4/Sub.2/1992/35, 25 Jan. 1992.

United Nations Human Rights Committee, General Comments: UN doc. CCPR/C/21/Rev.1, 19 May 1989.

Usher, G., 'Children of Palestine,' *Race and Class*, vol. 32, no.4, April-June 1991.

Vines, Alex, *RENAMO: Terrorism in Mozambique*, London, 1991.

Veerman, Philip E., *The Rights of the Child and the Changing Image of Childhood*, Nijhoff, Dordrecht, 1992.

Walzer, M., *Just and Unjust Wars*, 1977.

Wilson, Heather A., *International Law and the Use of Force by National Liberation Movements*, Oxford, 1988.

Woods, Dorothea E., 'Children Bearing Military Arms', Quaker United Nations Office, Geneva, Nov.-Dec 1992.

Youngers, Coletta, 'Peru Under Scrutiny: Human Rights and U.S. Drug Policy', Washington Office on Latin America (WOLA) Briefing Series: Issues in International Drug Policy, Washington D.C., 13 Jan. 1992.

Index